DIAL AND TALK FOREIGN AT ONCE

"A fascinating and totally enjoyable read."
~ Mark Roman, author, *The Worst Man on Mars*

"It's like two sides of Frank Kusy: the fun, jokey side and his more serious, eloquent, intelligent side."
~ Julie Haigh, *Top 1000 Amazon Reviewer*

"I caught myself laughing out loud in many parts!"
~ Evelyn Marbut, *Amazon reviewer*

"The best so far of this author's series of offbeat, true life adventures in India. Witty, informative, and downright hilarious."
~ Joann Greene, *Amazon reviewer*

"Frank Kusy has a real knack for coming across the weird and wonderful wherever he goes. It really made me laugh."
~ Sdan, *Amazon reviewer*

"If you've been to India, are thinking of going to India, or, like me, just enjoy a good yarn from a fabulous raconteur, you'll love this book."
~ ChrissieB, *Amazon reviewer*

Also by Frank Kusy

Kevin and I in India

Rupee Millionaires

Too Young to be Old

Off The Beaten Track

Ginger the Gangster Cat

Ginger the Buddha Cat

All titles available from Grinning Bandit Books

Dial and Talk Foreign at Once

Frank Kusy

First published in 2016 by
Grinning Bandit Books
http://grinningbandit.webnode.com

The people and events in this book are portrayed as perceived and experienced by Frank Kusy. Some names have been changed for privacy reasons.

ISBN 978-0-9934047-1-9

Cover design by Amygdaladesign

DEDICATION

For my dear friend Caryl Williams, aka 'Mrs Bloggs'

Contents

Author's Note

Some travel writers are born, some are made, and some stumble into it by complete accident. At the end of 1985, when my first book 'Kevin and I in India' was accepted for publication, I had almost reconciled myself to returning to a 9 to 5 job in Social Services. But fate had other plans for me. 'A new publishing company, Cadogan Books, are setting up shop in London and looking for someone to write a travel guide on India,' my agent Carolyn phoned me up to say. 'Would you be interested?' It was all I could do to contain my excitement and pretend to consult my diary . But all was not cut and dried. Cadogan wanted experienced writers, and I was hardly one of those. For six long days I waited for the phone to ring again. And then...

Chapter 1

First Base

When the phone rang on New Year's Day, 1986, it was Paula. 'Hey Frank, you just got the go ahead on that India guide,' came the strident tones of my new gung-ho publisher. 'Only thing is, you've got to cover the whole country in just 66 days. Do you think you can do it?'

The word 'No!' should have sprung large from my lips. Instead, I had beamed confidently at the receiver and said, 'Yes, of course. When do I start?'

'We're flying you out on January 24th and hauling you back last day of March. And before you ask, it has to be 66 days, not one day more, because of the competition. Have you heard of Tony Wheeler's Lonely Planet guide?'

Of course I had. Tony's book had started out as a pink saddle stitched Wheeler's guide back in the 70s. It was now 'the bible' to every backpacker travelling to India.

'Well,' continued Paula, assuming my response. 'Lonely Planet have their revised India guide coming out for Christmas. I want to have ours out by at least the end of October. That means you getting final copy to me by July 1st. Oh, and one more thing: I want it to aim at a completely different market – not just the backpacker crowd, but the well-heeled "middle-of-the-road" traveller. Will that be a problem?'

'No problem at all,' I assured her, beaming confidently at the receiver again. 'Leave it to me.'

How deluded I was. Not only did I miss home the moment

I left it, but when I landed in Bombay three weeks later it was in the middle of a three day national holiday and not even the tourist office was open.

But that was not my main concern. My main concern was Paula's last words to me. 'Don't forget, Frank, I want something new and different. Don't bring me back any hippy rubbish.' That could be a problem. My one and only previous encounter with India – the year before, in the company of a colourful character called Kevin – had been undertaken on a penny poor shoestring basis. What did I know about well-groomed travellers with money to burn?

The charming P.R. lady at the 5-star Taj InterContinental hotel, where I turned up for an interview around noon, laughed when I told her my objective. 'There *is* no middle range of foreign traveller here in India,' she said with a tinkle in her voice. 'Visitors either live first class or on the base line, like hippies.'

I didn't have the nerve to tell her I had just spent my first few hours on Bombay soil in a roach infested hippy hostel called the 'Rex' round the corner. I also didn't have the nerve to phone Paula and tell her our project was doomed from the start.

My one hope was that Tony Wheeler's team of researchers were, as rumoured, not doing their job properly.

'Who is Tony Wheeler?' said the P.R. lady when I returned from my fruitless foray to find some tourist information.

'He's the founder of the Lonely Planet guide for foreign travellers on a budget. Have you not heard of it?'

'Oh, the guide for the hippies,' she sniffed with disdain. 'I have been working here since we opened, and not once have we seen one of his people. We probably would not let them in anyway. We have a strict dress code.'

Well, that was encouraging. I gave mental thanks to Anna, my girlfriend back home, for insisting I wear a decent pair of trousers and a clean shirt to India. Given the choice, I would have strolled in wearing a straw hat and a pair of tie-dye shorts.

Dear Anna, she had seen what a state I had returned in last year – two stones lighter, head shaven, and looking like a convict. Neat and orderly in every aspect of her life, she didn't want to be going out with a hippy slob. Two and a half years now, she had been trying to reform me and, as with my mother, she wasn't having much success.

As I traipsed dejectedly back to the Rex, I turned a corner and ran into somebody who *only* knew me as a hippy slob…Megan! Yes, my old travelling companion from last year. It was such an incredible coincidence that we just stood and stared at each other, unable to believe our eyes.

'Wow, what are you doing here?' I said, giving her a big hug.

'I've just flown in from Sydney,' said my lean, tanned Scottish friend, flashing me her familiar cheeky grin. 'Thought I'd give India a second chance before I return to the U.K. What are *you* doing here?'

'Erm…I'm researching a new travel guide on India. I've got to be in and out of the country in 66 days.'

Megan's grin widened. 'That's so *you*, Frank. I still remember you dragging Jenny and me round Rajasthan last year – we didn't stay in any one place longer than 24 hours.'

'I'm not going to be staying in some places longer than *six* hours this time,' I grinned back. 'I've got a carefully planned series of domestic flights which is going to be whipping me round India faster than a jackrabbit on diet pills.'

A look of profound doubt replaced Megan's grin. 'Plans?

In India? Don't you remember all the plans that went wrong last time?'

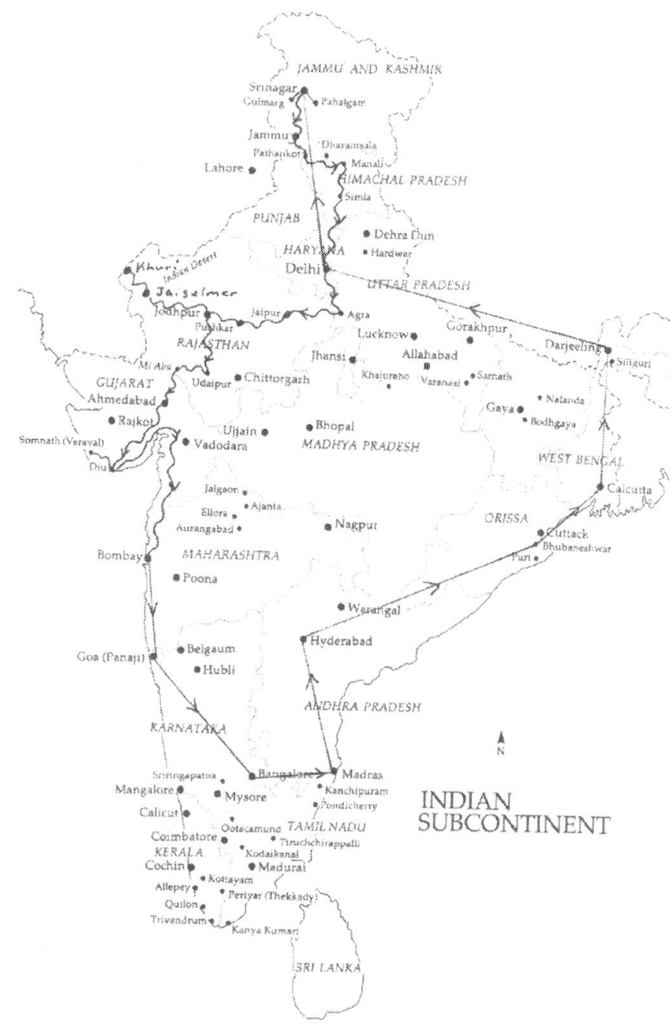

Well, yes, now that she mentioned it, I did remember. I particularly remembered planning a haircut for her in the small desert town of Pushkar and her emerging from the barbers'

shop practically bald.

Megan was not alone. A thin, vague-looking individual had just drifted up to her from a nearby book shop.

'Hi, I'm Steve,' he said, thrusting a short, stubby hand into mine. 'I heard the tail end of what you were saying. 'You a journalist or something?

'No, I'm a travel writer,' I replied. 'Though to be honest, I don't have a clue what I'm doing. This is my first day on the job.'

'Well, we got to celebrate that,' said Steve, a discernible Australian twang in his voice. 'And I know just the place. Let's go to Dipty's.'

But Dipty's threw me an unexpected curve ball. Just as we rounded the Taj hotel and the popular hippy juice bar came into sight, an oily young tout appeared out of nowhere and tugged urgently at my sleeve. 'Hey, Mister, change money? Good rate for you, 18 rupees to dollar!'

Eighteen rupees? That was twenty per cent more than the going bank rate!

My greed got the better of me. Without even thinking, I whipped out a hundred dollar note, thrust it into the tout's hands and whispered to Steve, 'Do me a favour, mate. Check what he gives you, while I keep an eye out for any chums he might have around who might be about to mug us. I don't trust this situation.'

I was right not to trust the situation. The tout pulled out a big roll of notes, began slowly counting them into Steve's hands, and then – as I got bored and wandered a bit too far away – shouted 'Watch out! Police!' And while we were all looking both ways at once, he legged it down a dark alley and was gone.

'This looks okay,' said Steve, passing the tout's money

over. 'Looks like a roll of hundred rupee notes to me.' But it was not okay. The top note was a hundred rupees, but the rest of the roll had been switched for measly ten rupee notes. I had been ripped off big time, lost about 80 dollars. And I had learnt an important life lesson. Never change money on the streets in India.

Chapter 2

Bombay Busted

By the time the tourist office finally opened its doors to me after the weekend, I had come to three significant discoveries.

First, I had come to really dislike Steve. Not only had he been suspiciously complicit in my getting ripped off (Kevin would never have fallen for that; Kevin would have counted the money in one hand and held the tout's neck with the other) but he also had a sneery, patronising attitude that made me want to pull out the hairs of his wispy little beard one by one. 'You want to get right round India in 66 days?' he'd scoffed when we finally sat down at Dipty's. 'You have no chance. Even if all of your carefully planned series of domestic flights go smoothly, which I very much doubt, something is bound to happen to trip you up. This is India, remember?' I'd only stopped hating Steve when someone broke into his locker at the Red Shield Guest House – where he and Megan were staying – and stole his camera. 'India is a lucky dip bag, man,' he'd sighed through his annoyance. 'Sometimes you get the sweetie. Sometimes you get the plastic spider.'

My second discovery concerned Megan. Shortly after absconding with her to far more comfortable lodgings opposite V.T. station and leaving Steve in the lurch ('He'll be okay,' said Megan. 'He's off to Manali tomorrow. I'll be surprised if we ever see him again') I caught a glimpse of her sizeable breasts in the shower. This had quite a mesmeric effect on me, and I was not the only one. Megan went straight from the shower to buy some chocolate and was followed all up the road by smirking Indians brandishing giant balloons in her face, and tweaking them suggestively. Then, the same evening, the hotel laid on a 'disco party' on the roof and she made the huge mistake of dragging some puzzled local onto the dancefloor. Next second, he had both his hands on her boobs. 'He looked lonely, and I felt sorry for him,' she said as she stormed off the floor. 'Well, what did you expect?' I laughed. 'You just don't do that sort of thing in India!' Poor Megan. She was no beauty, with her short, cropped hair and square, almost masculine jaw, but she did have an impressive chest and it did get an inordinate amount of attention from the Indians. Why she had made it so available to one of them was past my understanding.

My third discovery was most significant of all. After tramping the hot, sweltering streets of Bombay for four days, I had found just one mid-range hotel – the Hotel Diplomat in

Mereweather Rd – which I could recommend in my book. This vexed me greatly. 'Where on Earth *are* middle-of-the-road travellers supposed to go in Bombay?' I thought to myself. 'That P.R. lady at the Taj was right. There is absolutely no provision for them!'

I entered the tourist office with high hopes. At last I would be getting the 'real skinny' on Bombay, maybe even a cluster of hidden mid-range hotels. But my hopes were dashed. 'No, we cannot advise you on this matter,' said the tight-lipped Director lady. 'Also, we cannot offer free guided tours. You should have arranged this through the London office of the Government of India.' When I said there must be some misunderstanding, that I had already done two tours – one by bus around the city, the other a boat trip out to Elephanta Island – her rude reply was: 'Well, why else are you here?' I explained that a taped interview might be nice – I'd like to hear her personal view on Bombay – but she did not want to be interviewed. Instead, she snapped her fingers and commanded her subordinates to bring me a heap of very old and out of date information brochures which, she told me, 'had everything I needed to know' in them.

Disgruntled, I returned to the Taj, where the hospitality lady gave me a full tour of the hotel and showed me how *top* of the road travellers lived. My, what a difference! If you had a hundred dollars a night to burn, you got the full treatment – the marvellous swimming pool with nightly barbecues and parties, the famous health centre with gym for men and beauty parlour for ladies, the resident astrologer, the panoramic sea views from the top of the new skyscraper block, plus of course the prestige of staying at one of the world's best 12 hotels.

'You'll be our guest when you come back to Bombay, won't you?' said my smiley guide as we came to the end of the tour. 'Where would you like to stay: the Douglas Fairbanks suite or the Barbara Cartland suite?'

I looked at both suites and went for Duggie immediately. Not only was it festooned with rare and colourful posters of Mr Fairbanks in his dashing days as a silent movie star, but everything in the Barbara Cartland suite was pink. Right down to the pink telephone and pink ashtray. Somehow, I didn't think I'd sleep a wink in pink.

My next stop was the soaring Oberoi Bombay hotel which had just set up shop on Nariman Point. The tallest building in India, with 35 storeys, it sported the most sumptuous reception lounge imaginable, six speciality restaurants, massive swimming pool, high-rise landscaped gardens, vast shopping arcade, and the most exclusive disco in town. 'Guest arriving in dead of night are greeted by personal butler bearing gifts,' said the po-faced P.R. lady showing me around. 'Their first question will be: "Does Sir/Madam prefer the juice of the champagne?"'

'What a daft question,' was my first thought. Quickly followed by another: 'How is one supposed to see anything of the real India from here? This place is geared to top corporate business travellers, not at all for the kind of people I'm writing for. It's so big, that a major duty of the staff seems to be giving directions to lost residents!'

'I feel such a fraud,' I confessed to Megan later. 'Steve was right. Not only is 66 days not enough to cover the whole of India – I've just spent four days accomplishing virtually nothing in Bombay – but I just don't feel comfortable wandering through these big hotels in my increasingly dusty and crumpled white shirt and black trousers. I keep expecting to be thrown out as an imposter.'

'Oh, you'll be alright, Frank,' Megan consoled me. 'You have your Press card, you have that letter of introduction from Cadogan Books, and most important of all, you have that Walkman which you keep waving in people's faces. They've got to take you seriously.'

'Hmm, I'm not so sure about that Walkman,' I replied. 'It shut up that Director lady at the tourist office earlier, and the P.R. lady at the Oberoi looked at it as though it was some kind of FBI bugging device. I'm getting the distinct impression that high-ups in India don't like being taped. They probably think I'm a hack journalist who will do a big and unpleasant "expose" of them as soon as I get back home.'

Megan laughed. 'Could be, Frank. Maybe keep it out of sight from now on. It doesn't have to be jammed up their left nostrils, does it?'

To celebrate our last evening together, we left our cosy but stuffy little room and escaped to the wonderfully air-conditioned Empire cinema near V.T. station to watch one of the latest Bollywood epics. 'Bombay is the film capital of

India and produces more films than the real Hollywood,' I informed Megan. 'So we might as well see what all the fuss is about.'

This film was a real treat. A non stop extravaganza of colour and excitement, every few minutes the action would stop for a song and a dance. The hero and heroine were both plump, which struck us as reflecting the ideal in a country where most people were very thin. We'd both seen Hindi movies before, but it still surprised us that kissing was not allowed on screen. As a compromise, the two lovers moved toward each other, the music heightened to a crescendo, and at the last possible moment the film broke off into a montage of glorious symbolic scenery – blossoming flowers, gushing fountains and torrents of monsoon rain. Taken as a whole, it was a fascinating blend of Hitchcock, James Bond and 1930s screwball comedy. The intermission was quite brilliantly managed, an unseen pair of hands pushing the stout heroine off a cliff, the curtains closing, and the lights coming on all in the same moment. We returned to the cinema after the break to find the leading lady resting safely in a hospital bed – no clue was given as to how she had avoided her watery grave.

During the intermission Megan showed me a postcard she'd received from a friend in Agra. 'Hi Megan,' it read. 'I've just been handed a letter from a tout on Agra station. It said: "This is Ram. He was very helpful to me in Agra. He is very gymnastic and athletic in bed. I am sure you will be satisfied."

Further amusement was afforded us as we came to a zebra crossing along Veer Nariman Road. HOP ALONG IN LIFE said the road sign. OR CROSS THE ROAD CAREFULLY. 'The dogs of Bombay could do with reading that,' grinned Megan. 'Quite a few of them only have three legs.'

Our amusement didn't last long, however. 'Bombay is sign of our future,' our city bus tour guide had told us. 'It is go ahead city of tycoons, skyscrapers, film studios and big business. But there is one downside. All the poor people are flooding in at rate of 6000 new families per day. They come in search of work or glamour or money, and most of them end up sleeping on the streets. Where else can we put them?' It was a good question, and one Megan and I had been unable to answer. All that we knew, as we walked home from the cinema, was that we were regularly approached by incredibly pitiful beggars. Mostly mothers with emaciated infants who lived outside the Taj hotel, but also by lepers with missing limbs, roasted nut men, and kids desperately trying to sell us postcards or maps of India.

A comment from an old friend of mine, Peter Cork, came back to me now. 'Don't you feel pity when you who have so much are surrounded by those who have so little?' I hadn't felt much pity my first trip to India – I had been living on a budget of about 10 dollars a day and wasn't far from being one of the poor myself – but now, with a string of free flights and hotels in the offing, and with mid-range money in my pockets, something was beginning to change in me. The stirrings of real compassion, perhaps?

The night view from our top floor balcony back at our hotel was remarkable. The old and new of Bombay revealed themselves in startling dissonance: on the left, the palm-fronted, gothic GPO, faded and grey; on the right, the ghostly, white monolith tower of the ultra-modern Oberoi hotel, looming up like some kind of weird spaceship in the heart of an otherwise black, hopeless jungle. Staring at it through the mesh of TV aerials and the crush of tall slum tenements, I could only wonder at the stark contrast of poverty and wealth in this most modern of India's cities.

*

Early next morning, I saw Megan off on the 'fast express' train to Calcutta. This would be an astonishing 32 hour journey and I could see she was not looking forward to it. For one thing, her pre-booked 'ladies compartment' had just one occupant when we arrived – a solemn, owl-faced *man.* Ushering him politely out of the compartment, I sat down with Megan and shared a bag of soggy masala chips with her. 'Look, you're going to be in Darjeeling in a couple of weeks,' I said by way of cheering her up. 'What say we hook up there again?'

Megan's face visibly brightened. 'That would be wonderful! But bloomin' heck, Frank, that Walkman of yours is going to have to be working overtime for you to cover the whole of south and central India by then!'

'Leave it to me,' I said with every appearance of confidence. 'I've got two dozen cassette tapes in my bag . And a cluster of nippy flight destinations to fill them up in.'

In the back of my mind, however, I was not so confident.

Yes, my Buddhist mentor in the U.K, Dick Causton, had advised me to be like a sponge, to soak in all that was India and then to squeeze it all out again and produce something 'remarkable', but I was nearly a week into my stay in the country and I hadn't squeezed out a word! Panic struck my heart as I remembered Paula saying, 'I was a war correspondent in Afghanistan, we were used to pumping out 2000 words of hard copy a day.' She hadn't been to India, where heat, traffic, non-stop interviewing and endless distractions meant you were lucky to write a postcard!

Free of Megan, and feeling unexpectedly despondent, I began to think of home. In particular, of Anna whom – despite her warm and loving concern for me – I had left on a very uneasy footing. My previous book, 'Kevin and I in India', had almost split us up – the endless nights of me hunched over my typewriter had had Anna chewing the carpet. And her parting words to me at the airport a week or so earlier – 'Two months abroad and then three more months of isolation while you write a bloody guide? Call that a relationship, Mr Kusy?' – had hardly been encouraging.

But now, as I sat on the balcony of my cosy room and enjoyed a last breakfast in Bombay, I found time to put pen to paper (at last) and write to her, both warmly and in glowing terms about how beautiful this country was and how much I wished she could come see it for herself.

Part of me really meant that.

Chapter 3

Hallo Heepee!

I boarded the plane to Goa with some trepidation. Not only would this be the first time I would be travelling solo in India, but I had just remembered something.

Goa and I didn't get on.

We hadn't got on since I had last been here with Kevin. I had nearly fallen to my death from the top of a crumbling bell tower, someone had slipped me a joint of something called 'angel dust' and left me at the mercy of a pack of wild dogs, and a large pig had disturbed my toilet one morning by sneaking up on me in the bush and eagerly devouring my exuded faeces.

Perhaps it was the Jesuit association that made me allergic to Goa. The Portuguese Jesuits had arrived here in the 16th century – a sword in one hand, a crucifix in the other – and had made this a pretty grim place to live in. By the same token, I had suffered a pretty grim seven years of being physically and verbally lashed at a Jesuit school. The memories were still raw in my mind.

But it wasn't just the Jesuits. The whole commercial aspect of the place had bothered me: from the characterless 5-star package tourist hotels that were springing up along the beaches to the busloads of Indians that poured in every weekend to gawk at and take photographs of western hippy chicks who – for some reason – insisted on bathing topless.

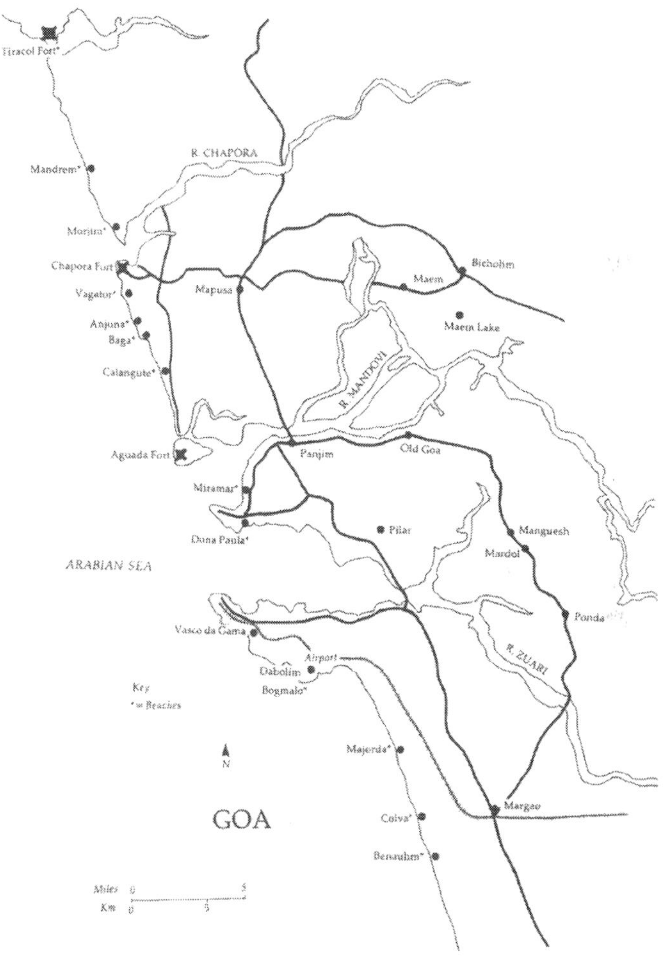

Off the plane, I headed straight for the Oberoi Bogmalo hotel on Bogmalo beach, a short five minute drive from the airport. Paula, my publisher, had cut a deal with the Oberoi hotel chain whereby, in return for positive reports, I would get to stay free in some of their establishments. Unfortunately, this was not one of them. The only freebie I got from the manager was a chilled beer, which – although appreciated – was not quite what I was hoping for. 'I am sorry we cannot accommodate you at this time.' he said snottily as he shunted me out into the street again. 'But this is high season, we have full occupancy.'

'Yeah, right,' I thought to myself. 'Well, I'll only recommend your beer, then.'

Goa was a massive place to cover – a long, narrow 100 kilometres of coastline with yes, some of the best beaches in the world, but at least a dozen busy, emerging resorts catering to them. The only way I was going to visit them all was by being bang in the centre of things. In short, I had to stay in Panjim.

Panjim was the capital of Goa and one of the least 'Indian' capital towns imaginable.

As I drove in on a slow and puttering local bus, I took in the legacy of its Portuguese past – the narrow, winding streets dotted with cafes, bars and tavernas, the Mediterranean-type town squares looking onto whitewashed, red-tiled houses, the distinctive red and yellow striped post boxes, the neat, flowery aromatic gardens, and the jolly toy-town helmets of the local policemen. It looked like a pleasant place to stay, and as soon as I hit the sleepy tourist office and recognised my situation, I was glad that the Oberoi had turned its nose up at me. Not only would I have had to shell out on expensive taxis to get anywhere from that distant resort, but the Panjim tourist office were offering two very useful sightseeing bus tours – one to North Goa, the other to the South – and both tours ran from practically outside my hotel.

My hotel – the Tourist Hostel – was apparently the best in town. This I found hard to believe. It was full of noisy, complaining Indian families on holiday from Bombay, and as I checked into my five dollar room I found a team of workmen dismantling a fridge right outside the door. 'You are so lucky,' a passing Polish backpacker informed me. 'This place is often booked out months in advance!' I considered my luck as my eyes took in my room – the high ceilings, stark white walls, and bleak décor were a depressing prospect. But then I found the wonderful iron-trellised balcony, which looked over rows and rows of gently swaying palm trees. 'What a great place for chanting,' I thought to myself. 'And I'm on the top floor, with a perfect view of the sunset!'

An uneasy evening followed, however. I had a contact in Panjim – a certain Mr Costa –whose name had been given me by my Buddhist organisation in the U.K. I was quite looking forward to meeting Mr Costa, if only to chant to a *gohonzon* (Buddhist devotional scroll) for once and not to a greasy spot on a hotel wall.

'Hello, heepee!' Mr Costa's girl maid greeted me as I knocked at his door. I smiled at this. Ever since the hippies had found Goa back in the 60s, every Westerner not in a suit was considered a 'heepee'.

I wasn't smiling long. The next moment, a wild-eyed, gangling figure wearing a fez swept the maid aside and clasped me to his bosom like a long lost brother. 'You have come! You have come!' he enthused. 'It is like precious gift from the Buddhist gods!'

I surveyed the tall, nut brown man with more than a degree of alarm. 'Erm, thank you. I hope you didn't mind me calling you earlier. Were you having siesta?'

'No, no, no!' protested Mr Costa. 'I cannot sleep, I am so happy! Now, come, come, come. We must talk!'

Ushering me urgently past the neighbour's evil dog (it almost had my leg off), Mr Costa sat me down in a small back room packed full of Japanese mementos and furniture. Then, in a burst of machine-gun chatter he informed me that despite 12 years practice (10 of them in Japan) and curing himself of duodenal cancer, he had come up against a total block in Catholic-dominated Goa. 'Nobody want to hear about Buddhism here,' he bemoaned. 'And even my wife stop the practice. But now YOU come. You must stay with us. And tomorrow, I have a big meeting with local people – YOU will help me spread the word!'

I began to panic. I did not want to stay the night with this wildly overenthusiastic man. I also did not want to tackle total strangers on the subject of my Buddhism. Really, my Buddhist organisation should have told me that Mr Costa was the only practising member in Panjim. No, scratch that, the only practising member in the whole of *Goa*. And now he wanted me to play John the Baptist to his Messiah?

My first impulse was to cut and run. But then I decided to stick it out. 'Erm, I'm not sure I can take you up on that. I have a very busy schedule. Do you mind if we chant about it first?'

'Of course! That is first priority! But I am sure you will help me! This is first proof of the practice I have two years!'

Chanting with Mr Costa was like chasing an express train. I just couldn't follow him at all. And right in the middle of it, his wife – a stout Japanese lady in her late 30s – came in and threw a flower pot at his head. 'You are making too much noise!' she complained. 'Shut up, or I cannot sleep!'

Afterwards, having reconciled myself to having done the worst *gongyo* (liturgy prayer) of my life, I summoned up all my courage and took Mr Costa to task. 'Please don't think me rude,' I said. 'But there's a saying in our Buddhism that if you befriend someone and lack the compassion to correct him, then you are in fact his enemy. What is your *gohonzon* – the supreme reflection of your life in the Buddha state – doing in this poky back room? It should be taking pride of place in this large house of yours! Also, if you know your wife is sleeping next door, why are you booming away like a big elephant?'

Mr Costa's brows knitted unhappily. 'Does this mean that you will not be taking up my offer of hospitality?'

'No, I'm afraid I won't. And look, I'd like to help you, but I have a full day bus tour tomorrow that is important to my work. What I will do, however, is chant that you have a very successful meeting.'

Mr Costa shrugged in token gratitude. 'Can nothing persuade you to stay a little longer?'

'Well...,' I said, detaching a piece of broken flowerpot from my shoulder and fishing out my Walkman. 'Do you mind if I ask you a few questions for my book? For instance, what do the Goan people feel about tourism? Do they feel it a good thing or a bad thing?'

'Tourism brings degradation,' was Mr Costa's tired verdict. 'Drugs, pimping, gambling, touting – all these things come around. Police are doing something now, but it is too little and too late.'

'What's this I hear about Goa losing her independence next year?' was my next question. 'Is she really about to become the 25th state of India?'

This question had Mr Costa's face turning a strange shade of purple. 'I know I should not say this as a Buddhist, but the Indians are coming and taking all our land! Over the last 10 years, our population has doubled – it is getting all crowded, not only with tourists but with financial sharks from elsewhere in the country buying up all our land. It is not good for the Goan people, you know – we'll be submerged as a minority. Even our culture is being wiped out. After 20 years, you'll find nothing of it!'

As I left my strange host's house, still feeling unsettled about the whole encounter, I wondered what Mr Costa was getting so worked up about.

According to one of the tour operators I'd interviewed earlier, the Indians had done a lot more for Goa than the Portuguese had ever done. Since their 'token invasion' in 1961, Goa had never had it so good. The Indians had installed electricity, turned bullock tracks into roads, and connected up North and South Goa with a series of bridges. Then they had developed the Pilar Harbour, a supremely fortunate combination of vast natural harbour backing onto a rich mountain of iron ore. Result? Goa had become rich practically overnight, and although I appreciated Mr Costa's concerns, the past 24 years of Indian rule had hardly touched Goa's old Portuguese character and flavour. As far as I could see, it was still a sleepy, laid-back Lisbon of the East.

Then I had a deeper reflection. Was I really doing Goa a favour by writing about it and encouraging others to follow me, via my guide? Tourism was both a curse and a blessing. Yes, it was bringing money into Goa and helping a cultural exchange between people from different parts of the world, but I couldn't help but feel uneasy that I was part of the downside of tourism – that I was contributing to changes in Mr Costa's beautiful old Goa and to the 'invasion' of which he spoke.

*

As I stabbed miserably at my SCREAM BLED EGGS and JAM TOST the next morning, I fell to mulling over what I would do if my travel guide ever saw the light of day. What I would *not* be doing, I inwardly determined, would be any more radio interviews. The radio tour that my 'Kevin and I' publisher, Jean Luc, had organised for me had not gone well. The first interview was cancelled at the last minute, the second, my crippling shyness had me stuttering all over the place, and the third was a complete disaster – I ran into Radio Oxford shouting: 'Bleep, bleep, bleep! I'm so bleeping sorry! The bleeping train was an hour late!' Only to be confronted by a DJ in the sound booth waving his arms about frantically and mouthing: "You're live! You're live on air to 45,000 people!"

Yes, live on air. And 'bleep' was not exactly the word I used.

From my miserable breakfast I went to some miserable chanting in my room. Poor Mr Costa, I felt so sorry for him. Half of Goa were hardened Hindus, the other half hardened Catholics. What chance did he have, one sad, lonely Nichiren Buddhist, of getting his message – that all people could achieve Buddhahood, or absolute happiness, in this lifetime – across to them? It was such a massive responsibility, and I chanted with grim determination that he might prevail.

An hour or so later, my misery deepened as the South Goa bus tour I was on dropped me off at the Portuguese ex-capital of Old Goa, The dark, looming Catholic churches – abandoned in 1835 following a series of nasty plagues – brought back memories of the seven unhappiest years of my life in a similarly dark, looming Jesuit college. 'I want you to have the best education in the world,' my mother had told me firmly. 'And I'm going to make sure of it.' My final damning school report – 'Francis only does well in the subjects he likes. This will doom him to failure in future life' – showed her how misguided that idea had been.

The only thing in Old Goa that provided a modicum of amusement was the shrivelled corpse of a much more successful Francis – St Francis Xavier – in the Basilica of Bom Jesus. 'Look the head!' commanded the excitable (and obviously Catholic) tour guide. 'It is untouched by time, like a miracle!' I gazed in wonder at the bald, mottled head in its silver casket. It did indeed appear remarkably well preserved. But it was not the defunct saint's head that concerned me – it was the rest of him. Perhaps the most well-travelled corpse in history (Xavier 'commuted' all over the place after his death in China in 1552), one of his toes had been bitten off by a Portuguese holy-relic hunter, some Japanese Jesuits had taken one of his hands, various sections of his intestines had been removed, and to top it all off, he had suffered a broken neck after being stuffed in an undersized grave. 'Blimey,' I thought to myself. 'Who'd be a saint?'

At the end of the tour, which took me on to – among other places – the unbroken 20 kilometres of near-virgin sands that was Colva beach and the quiet, secluded beach of Benaulim beach with its pretty little fishing village, I put in a quick call to Mr Costa – fully expecting a dejected response, if no response at all. On the contrary, he sounded quite chipper. 'I tell you tomorrow!' he said mysteriously, then put down the phone.

*

The next day was a Saturday, and my second bus tour – the one to North Goa – was packed full of Indian men. Where were they going? They were going to photograph Western women on the beaches, of course. Some of them couldn't even wait that long. One girl getting off a different bus at our first stop, Calangute, was greeted by an oily character who said: 'Hello! What do you think of sex? Twenty four hours a day,

I'm a powerhouse!' She got straight back on the bus.

Calangute, the old Queen Beach of Goa, where coconut palms once shaded a mile-wide stretch of tranquil sands, was now a fully-fledged Indian holiday resort and the top hot spot for camera-clicking voyeurs. Walking back from all the popcorn stands and iced beer stalls, I came across a lone Westerner – a rather sultry Italian girl – sitting on her own in a café. 'I hope you don't mind me asking,' I said. 'But I hear it's not safe, bathing topless on this beach.' Her look told me everything. 'No, it is not safe, especially at the weekend. My friend, she go topless this morning. She has nice swim, then she fall asleep on the beach. When she wake up, she think: "Where has the sun gone? Why am I in shadows?" Then she look up and she is surrounded by twelve Indian young-men, all of them grinning at her and pulling at the things in their trousers."

Next up was the freak beach of Anjuna, famous for its Wednesday flea market. According to Megan, this was where you came to buy your mirrored topi hat, your funky beachwear, your hippy bag and beads, and your chunky ethnic jewellery. 'The idea here,' she'd said, 'is to make yourself look like you've been in India six months and not six days.'

I was sorry to have missed the flea market – it was apparently like Woodstock on the beach – but this being a Saturday, it was still packed out with visitors. Not just a colourful mix of traders (mainly Kashmiris, Tibetans, and Gujarati tribals) but also with busloads of curious Indians. 'It's all going to hell, man,' sighed one guy I interviewed. 'I was watched having breakfast by 27 Indians.' This apart, there was no denying the whole buzz of the place – a wild, heady brew of astrologers, tarot readers, massage tents, throbbing sound systems, good veggie eats and lots of people sitting around on grass mats just taking in the scene.

I liked it.

I also liked the more northern beaches of Chapora, Vagator, and Arambol where I was told that people only roused themselves for mass bingo (with disco music) in the day and for open-air parties at night. 'I could do with a piece of that,' I thought wistfully. 'Instead of leaping on and off buses to quickly gather information at every stop.'

It was while on the long 4-hour drive back to Panjim that I

gave up completely on Paula's idea for a 'different' kind of guidebook to India, one aimed at the middle range of traveller. If Bombay had few hotels in the mid range, Goa had none. Wherever I went, the beaches were lined with a few poor huts inhabited by happy hippies strumming guitars or lying in hammocks. Not a two star, let alone a five star, hotel in sight. The only exceptions to this, as far as I could tell, were the rich-kid beaches of Fort Aguada and Bogmalo, where the Taj and Oberoi groups had set up shop.

Then I had the germ of a brilliant new idea of how to make my book different. If I was stumbling about India, with hardly a clue of how to structure my day so that I got the best out of it, how much more difficult would it be for the average first-time Western visitor? The 'sneak previews' provided by Government of India tour buses had been of such great use in helping me select the best sights to see in Bombay and the best beaches to visit in Goa. Why couldn't I apply these half and full day sightseeing tours to the rest of India? Okay, the government bus tours only ran in the bigger towns and cities, but I felt pretty sure I could break up the smaller places into easy-to-manage half and full day 'itineraries' by auto-rickshaws, cycle rickshaws, or even by foot if necessary. Something in the chaotic, mismanaged recesses of my mind began to take shape.

Back in Panjim, I met up again with Mr Costa at the Tourist Hostel's marvellous Chit Chat restaurant. Scanning the menu – which included a section of RAVISHING TANDOORIES – I briefly considered the famous Goan *chorrisos* (I was rather partial to a sausage) but then I remembered the pigs' diet in these parts and opted for a (delicious) Spanish omelette instead.

Mr Costa was in no mood for eating. 'Twenty people come

to meeting last night!' he exulted. Big success!' I congratulated him, and asked him what might be responsible for the sudden change in his fortunes. 'I do as you say,' came his perky response. 'First, I apologise to my wife for my bad behaviour. Then I move my *gohonzon* out of "poky back room" and put it in the brightest room in the house. To my surprise, my wife immediately say she will start chanting again and will support my meeting. She say she has been waiting for me to do this for years!'

I was so happy for Mr Costa. And in our shared happiness, I changed my opinion of Goa. Yes, it was somewhat short on laughs and yes, it was quickly filling up with (mainly German) tourists, but I couldn't take away from the very relaxed, slow pace of life. Or from the friendly, laidback people. One day, I determined, I would come back and do what so many other travellers did – switch off, put my feet up, and take a break from the 'real' India.

Chapter 4

Soft Wear City

Something occurred to me while I boarded the tiny 44-seater plane on to Bangalore. These past few days, I had been talking to a lot of total strangers. Why was this strange? Well, I had a deep fear of talking to total strangers – even working two years as a care home manager in South London hadn't got me over it. But here, on the other side of the world, with a lot more to be fearful of, I was approaching and chatting to dozens of complete strangers every day. Part of that, I guess, had to do with being on my own, with no Kevin or Megan to bounce ideas and conversation off. A much greater part, however, had to do with having a reason to talk to new people – my 'Frank Kusy – Travel Writer' business cards from Paula gave me carte blanche to interview practically anyone, from bigwigs in 5 star hotels to the lowliest type of 'untouchable' street cleaner. Day by day, I felt myself growing in confidence.

Off the plane, and bussing it into Bangalore, I found much to enjoy. It was lovely and cool, the city being 1000 metres above sea level, and very quiet too since it was a Sunday. The long, broad avenues were surprisingly clean and well-ordered, and the public buildings – particularly the palatial post office, the grand, red-brick Law Courts, the distinguished Parliament House, and the spic and span railway station – were most impressive. Bruised and battered from my intense experience of Goa, I felt a distinct lack of pressure here and began to relax.

Megan had recommended the cheap and popular Sudha Lodge in Cottonpet Main Rd as a good place to stay, and I duly checked in. Five minutes later – my room having been invaded by inquisitive roomboys wanting to buy my watch, whisky and calculator – I nearly checked out again. It was only when I offered them my left hand (the one generally used for toilet duty) that they all scattered.

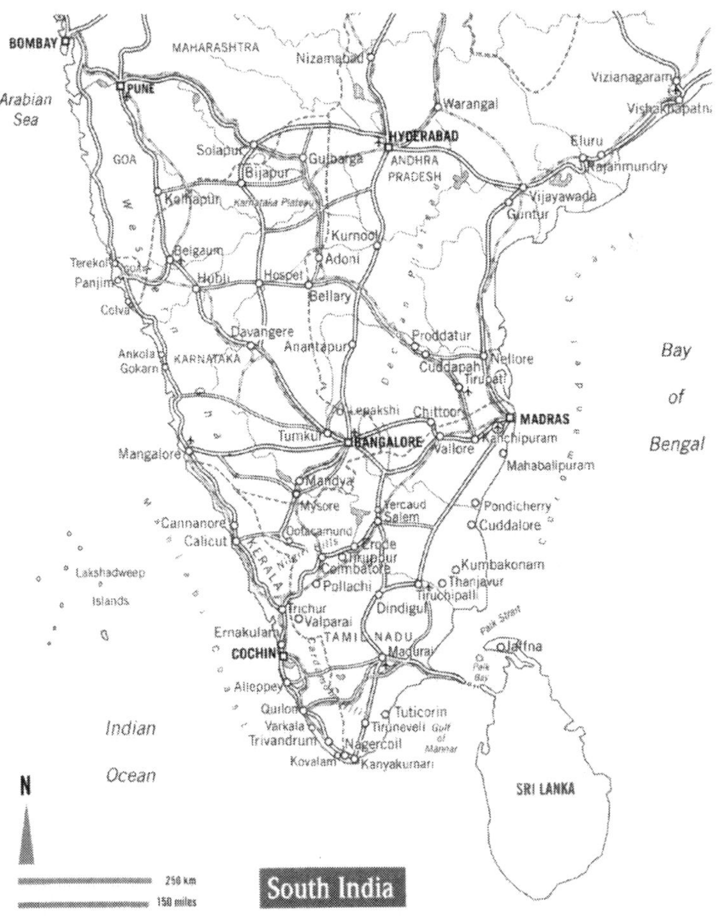

South India

Falling onto my bed and collecting my thoughts, I tried to remind myself what I was doing in Bangalore. Okay, it was the 'Garden City' of India (and its tidiest and greenest capital) but it was hardly a tourist hot spot. Then it came back to me. Bangalore was the jump off point to a number of other tourist hot spots – the fantastical abandoned city of Hampi, the wildlife 'tiger' sanctuary of Nagarhole, the charming Raj-style hill station of Ootacamund and of course the nearby royal city of Mysore. I wouldn't have time to visit all of these places myself, so I would have to rely on the Bangalore tourist office for maps and information.

Fortunately, I didn't need the tourist offices. Having rested up a while, I got everything I needed from Higginbotham's bookshop inside the clean, airy city railway station. It was typical Indian pot luck – there I was, waiting for my tour bus of the city to turn up and just killing time, and all the tourist literature on the whole of Karnataka state – up-to-date maps, bus and train timetables, flight timings etc –just fell into my lap.

The Bangalore tour itself was a disappointment. We didn't stop at the eye-catching Parliament building, nor at the lush, green grounds of Cubbon Park, nor even at the striking 300-year old temple next to the dull, old wooden Summer Palace of Tipu 'Scourge of the Raj' Sultan. What we *did* see was a murky lake, a so-so art gallery, and an unusually large *nandi* bull statue (dedicated to Shiva) up on Bugle Hill. Only when we came to the amazing giant 'glass house' in Lal Bagh – an elegant, vivid-green structure modelled on London's Crystal Palace – did my interest peak. It brought back memories of my childhood, when I had played amongst the ruins of the original Palace which had burnt down in 1936.

The tour bus to Mysore the next day was better. This time I was the only Westerner on board, and I wasn't on board for very long. The bus was double booked, and since I was the last to get on (having a last crafty fag as usual), I was first to be thrown off. Then I was allowed back in again and put in the back seat. Which happened to be a good thing. Now I could smoke without causing a nuisance. I also had constant access to the bus tour guide, who also sat at the back.

'I am very excited!' he said as we roared away on our marathon trip. 'Texas Instruments come to Bangalore last year. We are becoming software city!

Texans? Soft wear city? What was he talking about?

'You do not understand,' said the smart young man when I speculated that Bangalore was about to make fleecy boots for rodeo riders. 'Software is computers. First come Texan Instruments, then come many more multinational corporations. Rest of India does not know or care what is going on. These guys are writing new future for Bangalore. We will become big technologies!'

I still had no idea what he was talking about, but nodded indulgently. If he wanted to believe that calm and leafy Bangalore was going to turn into some kind of futuristic Star Wars cyber city, who was I to disillusion him? (*note: from 'Silicon city' of the 90s, Bangalore is now well on its way to replacing Bombay as the cosmopolitan and commercial centre of India.)

The tour was over-ambitious. Even the first stop – the ruins of Srirandapatna, ten miles out of Mysore – merited a full day's sightseeing. From this small island fortress-town straddling the river Cauvery, the two brilliant Muslim leaders – Hyder Ali and his son Tipu Sultan – ruled a powerful empire, comprising much of Southern India, for 40 years. Tipu Sultan, the 'Tiger of Mysore', became the most dreaded foe of the British in the South, and inflicted two punishing defeats on the forces of the East India Company before at last being overcome in 1799. The beautiful fort was destroyed but the elegant Summer Palace remained intact. Set in beautiful gardens, the stylish lime-green palace – built in 1784 in the Indo-Islamic style – was mainly constructed of wood and had one of the most beautifully painted interiors I had ever seen.

Not that I saw much of them. We were chased in and out of the palace like criminals on the run, our nippy young guide being interested in showing us just one thing – the place where Tipu Sultan had died. 'See, here!' he jabbered as he showed us a small plaque just out of town. 'This is where the British find our Tipu! He kill many before he is dying! He is lying under 50 redcoats or more!'

A short stop at Chamundi Hill, where we were shown an even bigger *Nandi* bull than the one at Bangalore, was followed by the main attraction – the huge Indo-Saracenic Maharajah's Palace at Mysore. A gleaming profusion of domes, turrets, archways and colonnades, it was designed by the English architect Henry Irwin and was built over a period of 15 years (1897-1912) after the old wooden palace was razed by fire. As I explored the Pandora's box of treasures within – the jewel-studded throne in the Durbar Hall, the mosaic marble floors, the stained-glass domed ceiling, the hammered silver doors opening onto sumptuously furnished apartments, and of course the mirror-spangled pleasure rooms – I remembered something Megan had said. 'You've got to visit on a Sunday night, Frank! The palace is brilliantly illuminated with thousands of tiny bulbs, there's teeming crowds of Indians having their picnics on the grass or milling about buying fruit and sweetmeats, and in the background mystic traditional music floats out from loudspeakers. The atmosphere is quite magical!'

Well, I wasn't here on a Sunday night, but I had seen my share of palace illuminations while I had been travelling with Kevin. Here, as elsewhere in India, the Maharajahs were making as much money from tourism – beautifying their palaces, and turning them into hotels – as they had before the coming of Independence in 1947 stripped them of their power.

The last stop on the tour was the best. I'd been adopted by a friendly family from Bikaner on the bus – they plied me constantly with coconut pieces, corn on the cob, and various drinks and sweets – and when we reached the fabulous Brindavan Gardens north of Mysore, they insisted on showing me around. 'This is where our god Krishna come to play with his 16,000 *gopigars!*' (handmaidens) said 'K.K', the large, bearded father of the group. 'One day last year, when schools break up, I count 400 tour buses coming here, all of them filled with young Indian couples wanting to play Krishna and *gopigar!'* Then, with a large sweep of his hand, he directed my gaze to the two kilometres of immaculately landscaped lawns, rose gardens, flower bowers and conifers leading on to the popular boating lake. 'This is like Taj Mahal in the South,' he said proudly. 'Have you not seen anything so beautiful?'

Well, no, I hadn't, and as I bathed in the collective joy of my adoptive family, I realised two things that had happened since I had left Megan. First, against all expectations, I had come to really appreciate travelling alone. Second, I was meeting lots of friendly Indian people and had been bowled over by their hospitality and generosity. 'This never happened last year with Kevin,' I mused. 'Travelling solo is obviously the way to go if I really want to touch base with the "real" India!'

*

Something I did not want to touch base with was the giant cockroach writhing on the floor of my room the next morning. It had been laid low by the insect powder I'd carefully strewn around my bed before retiring. Not for the first time, I found myself wrestling with my Buddhist principles. 'I am ushering it to the next and a better life,' one of my mentors in the U.K, Kazuo Fuji, had remarked as he carelessly trod on a beetle. When I protested, he explained that Man as a species had only survived by being a hunter. And he wouldn't have got far if he had gone the Jain route (Jainism was another offshoot form Hinduism, like Buddhism) and avoided treading on ants. Or by only hunting down vegetables. All that I knew was that I had grown up eating meat – my Hungarian mother was cook to Lady Astor, who really liked her meat – and that I had never seen a raw vegetable till I was sixteen. I also knew that if I was travelling in the wild, instead of populous cities, I could easily be hunted down and killed and eaten by lion, a jackal or a pack of hungry wolves. In the wild, anything was fair game and not so many mammals were vegetarians. 'Call yourself a Buddhist?' Steve had taunted me as I downed yet another tasty lamb kebab back in Bombay. 'Yes, I do,' I had told him rather tetchily. 'Even the Buddha ate meat. Leastways, he left strict instructions to his disciples on how to prepare it, so he can't have been adverse to the idea.'

But I still wasn't comfortable about killing cockroaches.

To make myself feel better, I phoned up Mr Anan, the local Nichiren Buddhist leader. 'Ah, so nice of you to call!' he said in a hard-to-pin-down accent. 'You must come visit with us!'

But visiting Mr Anan was easier said than done. The auto rickshaw I hailed had no idea where he was going. 'This is Bangalore's main problem,' I growled into my Walkman as we rounded the High Courts for the third time. 'It is too spread out, the streets are very long, there are few road signs, and even the houses rarely have their numbers clearly displayed. Who'd be a postman here?'

In the end, we only found Mr Anan by his own efforts. The man himself was standing in the street with a big sign saying:

'FRANK! I AM HERE!' It was hard to miss that. It was also hard to miss the fact that Mr Anan was not Indian as I had expected, but Japanese. 'Yes,' said the mild, bespectacled schoolmaster as he showed me through to his typically Japanese apartment. 'I come here from Osaka eight years ago for my work. I was the first person to chant Nam-myoho-renge-kyo in Bangalore. Now we have more than 50 strong members in the city.' He told me that his young men had contributed greatly to January's big Anti-Nuclear Exhibition in Delhi, which had drawn 16,000 visitors – a huge success for Indian kosen-rufu. (*peace in the land)

I did a good *gongyo* with Mr Anan and his wife, then – to overcome my washed-out feeling – I was permitted to use their *gohonzon* (Buddhist devotional scroll) for a great half-hour's chanting on my own. In the middle of this, without even being aware of it, I began admonishing myself for skipping on meals for days. 'I *must* eat sensibly,' I thought giddily, 'or pay the consequences.' I didn't have to wait long for the consequences. Seconds later, I doubled up with such a violent stomach-ache that I could hardly breath.

'How can you cure your illness if you do not take proper care of yourself?' Mrs Anan scolded me when I told her of my unintentional fast. She was quoting from the writings of Nichiren Daishonin, the 13th century sage whose teachings I followed. Then she spoon fed me some strange-smelling herbal tea until the urge to throw up on her carpet was gone. 'I'm so sorry,' I apologised afterwards. 'You won't be inviting any more U.K. members to your house in a hurry, will you?' Mr Anan laughed. 'No problem! They can come and expiate their karma with us any time!'

By now, I was feeling supremely confident about India. Feedback, contacts and information were now absolutely flooding in. Yes, my health was a concern and I could have done with a Kevin to bounce some humour off but I wasn't here for my amusement, I kept reminding myself. I was here to do a job, and so far, it had gone amazingly well.

Chapter 5

We even have Chaplin Charlies

Pride comes before a fall, they say, and so it was with me. Just as I thought I'd got a handle on India and was congratulating myself on the smooth progress of my travel guide, disaster struck.

The next day started well enough. I rose at 5am and enjoyed a beautiful sunrise on the short 45 minute flight east to Madras. Off the plane, the first thing I noticed was the heat. Madras was a *lot* hotter than Bangalore. The second thing I noticed were the friendly, dark-skinned Tamil people. Coming out of airport security and feeling in a generous mood, I laid a five dollar bill on a porter who flashed me a particularly happy grin. 'Thank *you,* sir!' he said, pummelling my hand. 'I am here on Mondays, Thursdays, and Saturdays!'

Nothing prepared me for what came next. I got the popular PTC bus from the airport into town, and then hopped on an auto rickshaw from Anna Salai Rd to Broadlands Lodge – 'the best hotel in India' according to Megan. Halfway to Broadlands, my heart stopped in my mouth. I had left my green shoulder bag – with my Walkman, camera, diary, and all my notes in it – on the airport bus!

'I lose my bag!' I urged the oily-haired rickshaw driver. 'Go back to airport!'

He looked at me as though I was joking. 'Go back? *No* go back! Bag is gone!'

'Bag is NOT gone!' I berated him. 'Go back to airport

NOW!'

A foolish giggle alerted me to the fact that this guy was quite crazy. Instead of turning back, he revved up his engine and ploughed forward with renewed ferocity. 'Bag is gone!' he began singing to himself. 'Bag is lonnnng gone!'

'Okay, that's it,' I thought with grim determination. 'This is my Waterloo. This the "something-bound-to-happen-to-trip-you-up" Steve had warned me about.' It was time to bring out the big guns.

'*Nam-myoho-renge-kyo!*' I screamed at the back of the driver's head. '*I want-my-bag-back-in-ten-minutes! Nam-myoho-renge-kyo!*'

That got his attention. The vehicle span round in such a drastic U turn that both of us nearly tipped out of it. Then, nine and a half minutes later, it screeched back up at the airport bus stop. And there was my bus. And there was the driver getting off of it. And there was my bag in his hands. And he was walking to a left luggage desk to hand it in.

My mad rickshaw guy couldn't believe it. 'This thing not happen in my life,' he marvelled. 'You are so lucky!'

'Luck?' I sniffed at him, thanking the bus driver and clutching my precious bag to my chest. 'Luck had nothing to do with it.'

Megan was right about the Broadlands Lodge. As I checked in with the friendly owner, Mr Kumar, I noticed all sorts of facilities that I hadn't seen in a budget lodge before – filtered drinking water, beautiful gardens bedecked with coconut fronds, a tourist information board, a lovely sun roof, even swing seats on the balcony to relax in the evening.

One special facility of the Broadlands was its cycle hire service, and it was here, as I planned a pleasant day's cycling round the city, that I ran into a young Welsh girl called Jessica. Slim and smiley, with an attractive bob of bleached, blonde hair, she was staying in the Broadlands' most popular room: the one with the famous graffiti wall decorations. 'I reserved it well ahead,' she said with a grin. 'It's a badge of honour among travellers to stay in room 18.'

Teaming up with her, we went to the Tamil Nadu tourist office in Anna Salai Rd – and got the most amazing reception. The Tourist Commissioner himself, Mr. R. Kirubhakaran, was visiting and he seized upon us like long lost relatives. 'I am new man on the job,' he said with a jovial wink. 'But I am going to shake things up. Have you seen our new features? We have videos, we have cartoons, we even have Chaplin Charlies!'

My eyes flitted around the busy office. A culture show video was playing, staff were fighting to answer ringing phones, brochures and maps were flying about, and everybody was *doing* something. 'This is amazing,' I confided to Jessica. 'This guy should be promoted to Minister of Tourism for the whole of India!'

As if he'd heard me, Mr. Kirubhakaran reappeared with a deluge of information, offered us all sorts of free tours, and even arranged for a limousine to drive us off to his favourite local restaurant. I made a mental note to give this man a special acknowledgment in my book – he was a testament to the true heart and hospitality of the Tamil people.

The (free) bus tour of Madras in the afternoon was a bit of a disappointment, but that was okay. I'd already visited some of the city's few sights with Kevin last year. I had also come to the conclusion that – with the exception of Georgetown to the north – Madras was best seen by bicycle, being largely on the flat and relatively free of the usual capital city traffic.

One thing, however, I had to show Jessica before leaving the tour. Leaving the Tamil guide for a minute (he was quite unintelligible) I drew her over to a curious exhibit I had spotted with Kevin in the weapons gallery in the Fort Museum. It was a weird little wooden cage in which a huge, whiskered officer called Captain Philip Anstruther spent a month after being captured by state guards in China in 1840 while on (East India) Company business. Anstruther was chained inside the cage, with a split open head, and displayed for the derision of the local Chinese until he received a miraculous pardon and was set free. 'For some reason,' I told Jess, 'he asked to keep the cage. And following his escape he apparently gave a beggar in the street a gold sovereign, exclaiming, "Good God, Man, you're the first man I've seen who's even uglier than me!"'

Back at the Broadlands, I spent a lot of time telling Jessica about Buddhism. About how Buddhism had been responsible for me coming to India for the first time last year (I had wanted to chant under the Bodhi Tree where the Buddha had achieved his enlightentment). And about how anyone could change their karma and attain *their* enlightenment in this lifetime, simply by chanting Nam-myoho-renge-kyo.

In return, Jessica regaled me with an account of her first day in Delhi. 'It is never a good idea', she said with a wry smirk, 'to stand around in India looking lost. Especially if you're an unattended female walking around on your own. I was lounging outside a shop in Paharganj when I was suddenly accosted by some bearded street astrologer. He grabbed hold of my arm and offered to read my palm. "This will only take moments, moments," he said, ignoring my struggles to get away, "You need to slow down, you are in too much hurry!" I told him to stop talking, that I wasn't going to give him any money, but he persisted nonetheless, saying: "You will be giving me money when you hear what I have to say." Too dazed and confused by my first contact with India to resist, I listened patiently as he scanned my tiny hand and came to a verdict. "You are nicely dressed," he informed me, "but I think you are a little insane. Yes, yes, you have positively lost your mind!" As if to emphasise this point, he began rapping his knuckles against my forehead until I literally saw stars. Then he produced a pack of playing cards with Indian gods on them and said, "What is your favourite colour? Take one picture. It will be the one you are most liking." But I didn't like *any* of the colours shown and simply replied: 'Yellow'. This produced a groan from the insistent Sikh. "Oh noooo!" he said. "It is the colour of the *insane!*" And he wouldn't accept my protestations to the contrary, just kept moaning that I had to spend more time with him in order to effect a cure. In the end, I had to empty every pocket, to show him I had no money on me, before he finally let me go.'

'How did he *know* you were insane?' I asked with a chuckle.

'Oh that's easy,' replied Jessica. 'According to him, I had nearly got run over lots of times. He saw it in my hands.'

I liked Jessica. She was fun to be with. She even indulged me when I suggested buying some beer and trying to find somewhere to drink it in 'dry' Madras where the consumption of alcohol was not allowed in public. A bizarre evening followed. We picked up our contraband – a couple of '5000' beers in brown paper bags – from a 'Wine' shop in Triplicane and then set out in search of the Hotel Sealord. This was apparently one of only a few hotels who would allow booze on the premises. 'I know Sealord!' said a diminutive, loquacious 'guide' who appeared out of nowhere. 'Follow me!' We duly followed on as he hopped and skipped in front of us and led us down some very strange little side streets until we were completely lost. Having picked our way over alley-fulls of sleeping bodies, goats, cows, beggars, vegetables vendors and through dark corridors full of haunted, hungry eyes, we lost the guide, found the Sealord by accident, and discovered that we couldn't drink the beer there after all. 'Drink beer possible at Hotel Sona,' chorused the Sealord staff. 'Sona very near!' But it wasn't. Forty minutes later, we reached the Sona and bounced back down the steps as the staff took umbrage at our bringing 'banned substance' into the place.

We ended up being pursued by two persistent students, one determined cycle rickshaw man (so keen to get our business that he rode onto the pavement and blocked our way), and an annoying 'genuine businessman' – all fighting over who would have the honour of directing us to the nearby Chinese restaurant. This was the *Chung King* in Mount Road – an old favourite of mine – where, having finally forced our way to it, we were only allowed to drink our beers provided we kept them concealed under the table, still wrapped in their brown prohibition-style paper bags.

Over food – a great meal of noodles, fried rice, chop suey and 'springs' rolls – Jessica asked me the big question I was hoping nobody would ask. 'So tell me, Frank,' she said. 'How do you expect to do justice to the whole of Tamil Nadu state, and in fact all the states you are covering in your book, when you are just landing in their capitals for a day or two and then flying out again?'

'Well,' I said, squirming in my seat. 'I'm only one person, not a team of six or eight people like Lonely Planet have. So I've got to cover six or eight times more ground in the same time. Guidebooks go quickly out of date, so a whistle-stop tour is the only answer. Besides, I've seen and *can* report on most of Tamil Nadu. I did most of it last year with my mate Kevin.'

Jessica gave a throaty chuckle. 'And I guess you can blag the rest of it – sorry, fill in the blanks – by hitting the tourist offices and talking to other travellers?'

'That's the general idea. Though there are some places I would love to have visited myself. Pondicherry, for instance.'

'Oh, I can fill you in on Pondicherry,' said Jessica, flicking back a stray lock of blonde hair. 'I was only there last week, and it's a crazy place. Pondicherry is basically an old colonial port town which was previously just for gurus but which quickly got taken over, in the Sixties, by western freaks and beach bums. I tried to get access to the Auroville ashram there, but was blocked by some French ponce who wanted to know *why* I wanted to go in. I replied that I wanted to see the Matrimandir, the huge hall they'd built inside. The Frenchman shook his head pityingly and said, "Actually, we don't *see* the

Matrimandir – we *feel* it!" I thought a moment and replied, "Okay, I've come to *feel* it then!" But this wasn't good enough for my French inquisitor – he wanted to know *what* I expected to feel in this place. I guessed "Meditation?" and was told, "No! Concentration! We *concentrate* in the Matrimandir." There was an Israeli waiting behind me. He must have been listening, because when they asked him why *he* wanted to enter, he said: "I want to *feel* it and I want to *concentrate* in it!" They let him in like a shot.'

*

The next day, I was woken by a lot of human traffic outside my window at 6.30am. Shortly after that, a room boy arrived with what he termed an 'omelette – actually, a boiled egg wrapped in a banana leaf. Five minutes later, he returned bearing a vacuum flask full of steaming hot coffee...but no cup. 'What is your name?' I enquired of the small, madly beaming urchin. 'Money!' came his happy response. 'Is that really his name?' I asked Mr Kumar over his shoulder. 'The boy on duty last night was called "Money" too.' Mr Kumar gave a patient waggle of the head. 'Oh yes,' he said. "Little Money" come, "Big Money" go!'

Over breakfast, I fell to reflecting on Madras. From what I had seen of it so far, it had to be the easiest and most pleasant introduction to India – far less noisy and stressful than overcrowded Delhi and Bombay. It also differed from those larger Indian capitals in three major respects. First, it was the home of the ancient Dravidian civilisation, hardly touched by the Aryan invasions of the North, and could claim to be 'pure' Indian. Next, it was unusually spacious – a wide, green and airy 30 square miles of parks and gardens, beaches and esplanades – with (as yet) very few built-up areas and a population of just 4.5 million. Last, it had managed to grow from rural village to modern metropolis in 350 years without losing its simple, small-town charm.

But what made Madras special were its people – dark-skinned, shock-haired, irrepressibly friendly Tamils with an obsessive love of foreigners. 'I saw a lot of the Tamils last year with Kevin,' I'd told Jessica earlier. 'And they have to be the most *curious* Indians by far. They stare and follow you about a lot. This is not rude. They just have no inhibitions, or any restrictions on "personal space" at all. A chance enquiry will, for example, attract a vast, swaying crowd of people within minutes. They are all just curious to see "what is going on."'

A prime example of this curiosity came this evening, when a car turned up to take Jessica and me to a huge complex of entertainments called the Fairlands Tourist Centre. The brainchild of Mr Kirubhakaran (who had sent the car) it housed a large fairground, lots of sideshows, culture and dance displays, various environmental and health exhibitions, and a miniature railway.

Hardly had we got out of the car when a bright-eyed young student sprang to my side and engaged me in a typical Tamil-style conversation:

'Hello,' said the student.

'Hello,' I replied.

'What is your name?'

'Meera nam Frank hai.'

'Ah, you speak Hindi!'

'Well, "thora", a little.' (I was trying to impress Jess here, but already regretting it)

'Ah, thora, thora...You are coming from?'

'England.'

'Which place England?'

'London.'

'London *proper?'*

'Yes, proper London.'

'You like our country?'

'Yes, *bahut acha,* number one!'

'You like cricket?'

'No.'

'Botham!'

'Yes, Ian Botham.'

'I have a friend in London. His name is Kumar. You know him?'

'London is a very big place.'

'You have English coins?'

'You have *Indian* coins?'

The student paused a moment, to consider his last gambit. 'You take my address,' he said. 'Send me photo. Come my house. It is near. We will talk cricket, Margaret Thatcher, sexy ladies, and whatnot.'

*

The following morning found me leaving the Broadlands and seeking out altogether more salubrious lodgings at the 3-star Oberoi Trident hotel. It did not go well. From the sidelines of the vast banqueting hall, seventeen waiters were hovering, their coal black eyes above starched white uniforms fixed on my isolated presence. Who would get to serve me first?

I did not have to wait long. The moment I withdrew a roll-up from my pocket there was a mad dash as all seventeen of them sprang into action and proferred seventeen lit cigarette lighters. I felt like a birthday cake.

I also felt very uncomfortable. For nearly two weeks now, I had been looking forward to my first bona fide free stay at a luxury hotel – a lovely, cool escape from the heat, dust, noise, and mosquitoes of India. Imagine my surprise then, when I appeared to be the only guest. 'Where are all the other guests?' I asked the manager when he came upon me in the banqueting hall. 'Oh, we are still building some things,' he replied, waving a casual arm at the busy lines of workers filing past. 'Did not Miss Levey inform you of this?' Well, no, Paula had told me nothing. All that I knew was that I was expected to recommend a hotel that hadn't been built yet.

What was I going to do? I'd been given the standard tour of the hotel – drinking in as I did so the five acres of tropical gardens, the three speciality restaurants, the pretty pool, and best of all, the wonderfully cool, air-conditioned room that had been lovingly prepared for me.

But it didn't feel right. I was missing having Jessica around, I couldn't sit in my room for more than ten minutes without feeling like a prince in exile, and all these waiters suddenly zoning in on me had made me jump out of my chair. Most important of all, I was parked in yet another Oberoi that was miles from anywhere (it was only convenient for the airport) and had a whole day ahead of me with nothing to do.

I came to a decision.

'What are you doing back here?' said Jessica, an amused smile playing on her thin, mischievous features. 'Couldn't you cut it with the rich and famous?'

'Something like that,' I replied sourly as I resigned myself to another hot, mosquito-infested night at the Broadlands. 'Are you still up for that cycling tour we talked about?'

'Sure thing,' said Jessica. 'I was hoping you could make it.'

.A long hour's cycling south took us to a series of pretty roads and 'English country' lanes – to the Theosophical Building founded in 1875 by the pioneers of comparative religions, philosophy and science, Annie Besant and Madame Blavatsky. Mysteriously shrouded in dense shubbery and creepers, this building opened up to a vast campus of beautiful grounds, shrines to all faiths, and one of the oldest banyan trees in the world.

Ten minutes later, we came to our objective – Elliot's Beach. The beach here was the best for miles, though as usual it was impossible to avoid attention. We tried to hide under a fishing boat but it was no good. Two grinning fishermen immediately popped up, determined to 'look after us'. Actually, they were real gentlemen – kept all the gawking riff raff away while Jessica peeled off and went swimming in a bikini. They also showed us lots of interesting sea crabs, even opening up one or two to reveal the red mass of 'eggs' inside.

At this point, another grinning individual appeared. This was a whiskered old rogue calling himself Johnny Walker who made his living by selling (beautiful) sea shells to tourists on the beach. 'No, I am telling you, ma!' he addressed Jess with his irresistible sales patter. 'These shells should be costing one million rupees, but no, ma, I am not asking for this!'

I shot Jessica a worried look. 'What's with the "ma" thing? I said in a hushed whisper. 'Are you related?'

'No,' she said with a tinkling laugh. 'Locals in Madras have a strange tendency of calling foreign ladies "Ma". A Japanese guy and me took over a cycle rickshaw a few days ago, because the driver was too old and tired to get up a hill. He observed us for a minute while my Japanese friend struggled to master the machine and I had a fit in the back, and then he hugged his sides with mirth and shouted: "Ha, ha, ha!

Pa is driving and Ma is laughing up behind!"'

Johnny Walker wanted to take us back to his home on the beach and put us up and treat us to food and refreshments. But then he showed us his big book of testimonials. 'Johnny Walker is an honourable guide, procurer, raconteur and companion,' he pointed us to his favourite one. 'If you want to see the real India, you will be unconditionally stimulated in his hands.'

This time it was Jessica's turn to shoot me a worried look.

After an invigorating swim in the bracing waves, we collected our bikes and made our way back to the Broadlands. Few words were spoken as we knew it would be our last night together. For Jess, not so bad, she'd be flying home to friends and family in a few days. For me, not so good. It had been so nice having some Western company again. All of a sudden, travelling more or less solo the next two months didn't have the same appeal.

But then, back at our lodge, Jess gave me something to look forward to. 'I can't understand it,' she said with a toss of her pretty head, 'but I've done more in the last three days than in the whole of the past month. I'll have to start chanting, Frank. You'll have to teach me!'

Somehow, I felt I hadn't seen the last of Jessica.

Chapter 6

Big on Zoos

The next day was critical. Come what may, I had to fly halfway round East India and cover the whole of Hyderabad – the fifth largest city in India – in just 10 hours. And after just two hours sleep.

I rose at 3.30am and did a stunned *gongyo*, then crawled over the sleeping bodies of Broadlands staff and got into my waiting taxi. The streets of Madras were eerily quiet this time in the morning – only two well-to-do Madrassi ladies waved to me from the dead pavements. I just caught a whiff of the sweet-smelling jasmine wound into their hair as I shot through to the airport.

Arriving in Hyderabad on a giant air-bus at 7am, I had a shock. It was a Sunday and everything, including the tourist office, was closed.

I gave myself a mental slap. How had I not foreseen this? How on Earth was I going to get any work done?

Following on from these two questions came a third. What was I doing in Hyderabad in the first place? Yes, it was capital of Andra Pradesh state and the fastest growing city in India, but its remote location meant that few tourists came here. Then my tired brain had a memory flash and one word clocked up – 'Zoo'. Hyderabad was supposed to have the best zoo in India. Paula was big on zoos. She had insisted on me seeing this one.

'Sir! Sir!' said the turbaned taxi driver outside the airport. 'Where you go?'

I did some frantic chanting inside my head. Where *could* I go at this unearthly time of the morning? It was too early to hit the big hotels and even the smaller ones were likely to be still asleep. In a moment of pure impulse, I pulled out my Lonely Planet guide (yes, I had brought the 'enemy' along) and stabbed a random finger at the section for Hyderabad.

'I go *here!'* I said, clambering into the taxi. 'Take me to hotel Rock Castle!'

It was a fortunate choice. The Rock Castle hotel was not only open, but it had a most interesting guest just checking in. The red beret cap and the gold buttoned black jacket gave him away. 'Excuse me,' I said. 'I'm a travel writer from U.K. and really need some help. Would you happen to be a tourist officer?'

'Yes, I am,' he replied, turning to me with a smile. 'You are in luck!'

The odds against finding the one and only off duty tourist officer in uniform – on a Sunday, and in a city of 6 million people – went way beyond luck. It had to be karma.

Over the next hour or so, my swarthy-faced saviour – Mr Choudhary by name – filled me in on just about everything I needed to know about Hyderabad. 'I am sorry I cannot give you personal tour of city,' he apologised as my Walkman clicked off. 'My wife she is expecting me. But I will send every printed informations to your address in U.K. Okay?'

Okay? That was definitely okay. Again, I had to pinch myself at my good fortune. As with my bag in Madras, the *shoten zenjin* – the protective forces of the universe – had turned up just when I needed them.

I now had time to see some sights, and they were a lot more impressive than I had expected. A chatty auto rickshaw guy – with a weird little mantra of 'No hurry, no worry, chicken curry!' – drove me out to Golconda, the huge fortress city from which the Muslims ruled their Hindu subjects until epidemics of plagues and cholera forced a move to Hyderabad in 1591. Though partly in ruins, this monumental fortress – which had taken the Persian Qu'tb Shahi kings – or rather, several thousand of their labourers, working day and night – 62 years to build stood on a picturesque hill and brought back a strong memory of the Alhambra in Granada, where my mother had once taken me as a child.

'Here! See!' said the cheerful Muslim guide I had engaged to show me round. 'Here is vault where Koh-I-Noor and such-much other famous diamond is stored!' Then he moved me on and made me clap my hands in the centre porch of the Grand Portico entry gate. 'You can get clap from here to top of fort – big acoustics!' was his dubious comment. Finally, having whizzed me through a maze of winding ruins, nooks and crannies, he directed me to a cranny he was particularly keen that I see. 'Here,' he whispered as we came to the royal kitchen on the site of the old Camel Stable. 'Here is something special!'

It was special alright. A strange smell not unlike buttered popcorn was emanating from the darker recesses of the kitchen. Following it, the smell was reinforced by a high chittering sound. One step further, and I found myself shrieking with terror. I was standing under what had to be one of the largest colonies of bats in India. 'Oh my *God*,' I panicked as squadrons of the nervous, flapping creatures wheeled and screeched around my head. 'That popcorn smell was bat shit! I HATE bats! Get me out of here!'

My giggling guide was unrepentant. 'Take photo? Bat is lucky!'

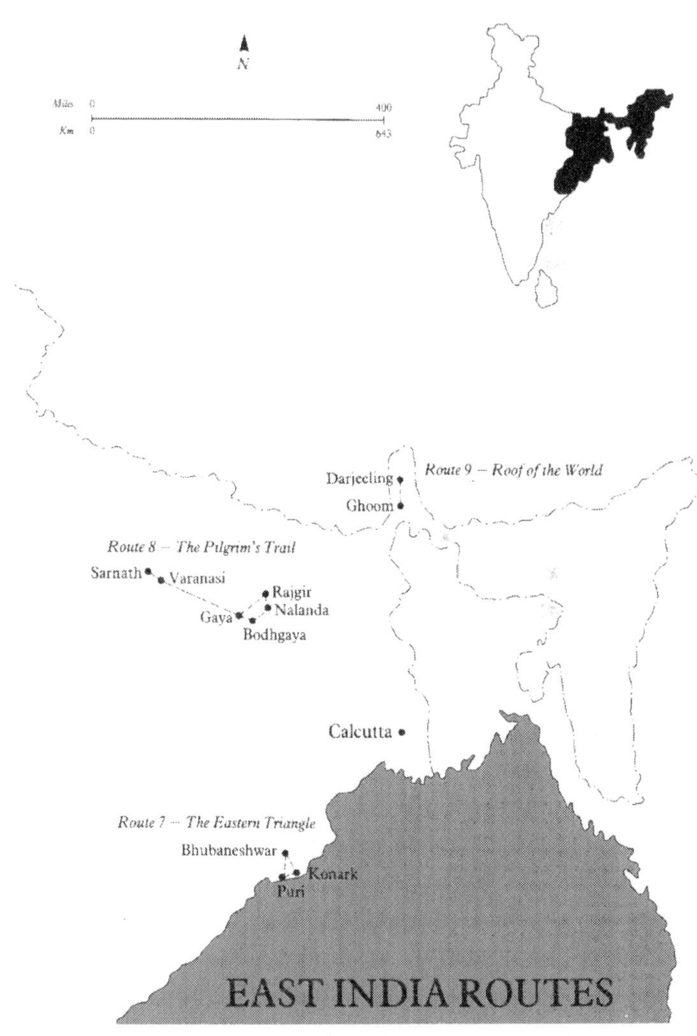

It was back in Hyderabad that I gave up completely on the idea of covering places by guided tours. I had heard for example that the guided city tour of Hyderabad allowed only one hour in Golconda. Absolutely ridiculous. Even going at lightning pace, I was there twice that long. From now on, I determined, I would try seeing places by cycle or rickshaw. After all, most big sights had a gang of good guides 'in situ' and I could choose one I could *understand.* Yes, I'd spend more, but I wouldn't be taken to any more obscure Indian temple or picnic spots and could stay in good places for as long as I liked, instead of being packed off in a tour bus after ten minutes.

The only drawback to touring Hyderabad city centre *not* on a tour bus, however, was the traffic. It was mind-bending. Looking down from the imposing arch of the Charminar, the city's definitive landmark, I took in the melee of overcrowded city buses, crazed auto-rickshaws which stopped for absolutely nothing, and a few maniacal taxis. DAYDREAMING IS DANGEROUS cautioned one traffic sign. MAKE UP YOUR MIND WHAT YOU ARE GOING TO DO, THEN CROSS THE ROAD.

I couldn't see many travellers getting around on foot.

Leaving my bag at the railway station cloakroom for just one rupee, and feeling much lighter, I moved on to the main attraction – the Nehru Zoological Park, a few clicks out of town. The rickshaw obeyed the meter (for once) and despite irresistible herds of giant water buffaloes crowding the highways we reached our objective – via a scenic vista of glittering palaces, mosques and lakes – in under 20 minutes.

Hyderabad zoo was beautiful. Unlike the one at Mysore, where the animals had looked fettered and unhappy, this vast complex (300 acres of it) had the space and facilities to give most animals at least the impression that they were living in their natural environment. Yes, the elephants were on chain leashes – I guess they had to be – but most other wildlife were running loose within large compounds, often with just a deep, narrow ditch separarating them from the tourists. 'You've *got* to come visit yourself!' I began composing a letter to Paula. 'This is perhaps the only zoo in India where the animals have enough room to run away when insensitive humans begin teasing and throwing buns at them. Oh, and get this, our bus broke down in the nearby Lion Safari Park and the lions wandered over to stare at us instead. They got so close, we could almost feel their breath on our faces!'

My second flight of the day was 1000 kms north-east to Bhubaneshwar, and it gave me plenty of time for reflection. The real joy of India, I silently mused, was not only experiencing it first-hand, but comparing one's experiences with other travellers. It helped to keep one's own experience in proportion. One also got a free exchange of useful up-to-date information – I learnt more about real Madras, for instance, by just hanging about the Broadlands reception area for an hour than a whole afternoon on a government tour bus. And even though I hadn't met any travellers in Hyderabad (there weren't any) I was now well-equipped to feed back to anyone I met who wanted to go there. Day by day, I was feeling more of a genuine travel writer and less of a clueless fraud.

That said, I still hadn't written a word for my book. Or written to, or called, Paula. I could virtually hear her screaming: 'Where's my *copy?'* I had devised 13 recommended 'routes' – each starting from the four capital cities of Bombay, Madras, Calcutta, and Delhi – and had prepared maps for these routes, but two obstacles stood in the way of my actually writing about them. First, my handwriting was so poor, I could hardly read it myself (Paula would have had no chance). Second, and this was more pertinent, I had set myself such a blistering pace – wearing myself to a frazzle in Goa, for instance, and catching a bad cold jumping on and off buses collecting information – that my Walkman had never stopped whirring long enough for me to breathe. Jessica had been a welcome tonic and I had been more than lucky in Hyderabad, but my joy at finally getting to grips with India was tempered by a growing guilt and despair at the mammoth task ahead of me. Sixteen days into my trip and my pen hadn't hit paper yet!

To make matters worse, my nose had started running like a tap. Very embarassing. Landing in Bhubaneshwar at 8.30pm, the milling mob of rickshaw men outside the airport recoiled at my miserable presence– my eyes were red raw with exhaustion and half a toilet roll was dripping from my streaming nostrils. And it wasn't just my eyes and nose that were in trouble. A whole day of travel in intense heat had me feeling like a sweaty, overheated radiator.

The first thing I did when I finally got a ride into town and checked into the spic and span Panthaniwas Tourist Bungalow (chosen because it was bang next door to the tourist office) was jump in a shower. The second thing I did was climb under my mosquito net (a most fortunate provision) and sink on spotless white sheets into a glorious nine hours sleep.

It had been a long, long day.

Chapter 7

The Coming of Norbert

I quite frightened myself with the hacking cough I woke up with the next morning. I sounded like a barking dog. 'This is no good,' I told my haggard reflection in a mirror. 'I *must* take better care of myself.'

To this end, I had a quiet, relaxing breakfast in the Panthaniwas's excellent Chinese restaurant and then, having done a strong, if rather croaky, *gongyo*, I decided to let myself be driven around all day instead of tramping the streets.

The chanting worked. A few steps out of the guest house I was adopted by a friendly, intelligent bicycle rickshaw man destined to become my all-in-one city guide, friend, and protective angel. 'My name Mohan Rao,' he greeted me with a winning smile. 'I am educated in six languages. I am bestest guide in Bhubaneshwar!'

I couldn't fault him on that. For just 60 rupees, he took me all round the city's extensive temple curcuit in the morning and all round its several hotels in the afternoon and evening – a long six and a half hour haul.

'We have fifty-six thousand foreign tourist this year!' Mohan said excitedly as we set out on our tour. 'Bhubaneshwar is coming on the map!'

Fifty-six thousand foreign tourists? This I found hard to believe. 'Don't you mean Indian tourists?' I quizzed him. 'I haven't seen a white face since I arrived.'

'No, no, no,' insisted Mohan, turning on his bike to shoot

me a toothy grin. 'Many Europe people come for see temples. Many Buddhist also!'

My ears pricked up. Buddhists? Oh yes, I remembered now. Bhubaneshwar was not only the capital of Orissa state, it was also the heartland of the ancient Kalingan empire which had been smashed so ruthlessly by the Mauryan king Ashoka that, having witnessed the wholesale carnage he had inflicted on the people, he converted to Buddhism.

Not that the Buddhist thing had lasted long, according to Mohan. The people's faith had soon switched to Jainism, and after that to the worship of Shiva. Consequently, the small group of 30 or so 'living' temples (shrines where the gods' 'lifeforce' was maintained by regular devotions) were all Hindu.

I had a bit of a problem with temples. I had been so templed out in India last year that I had told Kevin: 'If I have to see one more temple, I'll go live in a forest.'

I supposed I had to be grateful I wasn't around 500 years ago, when Bhubaneshwar had gained its moniker of the 'Temple City of India' and where 7000 sandstone temples stood on the site of the Bindusagar Lake alone.

'We see only six,' said Mohan soothingly when I confessed my temple allergy. 'Very nice temple. You like.'

The first of the huge, distinctive beehive–shaped temples I was shown belonged exclusively to Brahma. 'This is Brahmashwar temple,' Mohan informed me as he parked his bike under a huge banyan tree. 'Father Brahma live here to be *quiet*. All rest of family – Shiva, Ganesh, Parvati – live in big Lingaraja temple. That one very noisy!'

From the Brahma and Lingaraja temples, we moved on to the Rajarani temple ('No god live here, just dead Rajah and dead Rani'), then to the Mukteshwar temple, one of the most refined temples in Orissa. Even I was impressed by this one: it had an incredibly ornate entrance arch and elaborate carvings both within and without. Ringed by mango and jackfruit trees, it was also surrounded by Bhubaneshwar's small population of temple beggars.

'Hello, master, hello!' a beautiful boy beggar addressed me. He bore a striking resemblance to Tony Curtis and was shambling along on withered legs.

'What's his story?' I asked Mohan with more than a little concern in my voice.

'Polio,' shrugged my disinterested host. 'Family not have money for vaccine. It is common story.'

'Common story? Why have I not seen beggars anywhere else in city?'

'Bhubaneshwar is rich city,' said Mohan jokingly. 'Only poor man is me!'

Having visited both the ancient Parumeshwar temple round the beautiful Bindu Sagar lake and the famous 'black magic' Boital temple dedicated to Durga, I found myself talking to Mohan about Buddhism.

'You should try chanting,' I told him. 'It will make you feel good.'

'Okay,' he said. 'But what I pray for?'

I considered. This could go badly wrong. 'Well,' I said slowly. 'You tell me you can speak six languages, but you can't read. That's worth chanting for.'

Mohan nodded thoughfully. 'I start today!'

Around sunset, I took a pleasant ride out of town to the stylish 5-star Oberoi hotel, where the warm and friendly manager – Raju by name – welcomed me with open arms. 'Oh good, you come!' he boomed, his fat, jolly jowls wobbling with joy. 'Will you be staying with us?' My heart skipped a beat. 'I'd love to,' I replied. 'I haven't had much luck at the Oberois so far – do you really have you a room for me?' This made him laugh. 'Of course, but first, let me be asking you this, do you like *meat*?' I confessed that I did, and he slapped me on the back and said: 'Excellent! You must try one of our *steaks!'* Then he plumped me down in his plush new restaurant and said, 'What will be your pleasure?' Two weeks of near-vegetarian living fled behind me as I scanned the pure-carnivore menu of hot dogs, burgers and steaks. 'I'll have the *fillet mignon,'* I said, my mouth already watering. 'Good choice,' he said with a wink. 'This is *cow* meat, not buffalo!' I blinked. It was only a matter of time before he said that to the wrong person. But as if reading my thoughts, he laughed. 'Do not worry, my good fellow, the cow is not sacred in my hotel. I've eaten tons of the stuff!'

Moments later, he wasn't laughing any more. There was a power cut and the hotel was plunged into darkness. 'Oh dear,' apologised Raju. 'Your luck is out again. Two nights this week we are having these cuts. I think you must go back to the Panthaniwas – they have a back-up generator, we do not.'

The return ride to my guest house was spooky – the power cut had taken out the whole of Bhubaneshwar and its environs, and the only lights illuminating the otherwise pitch-black highway were the dozens of small, flickering oil lamps along the wayside which marked the 'patch' of various fresh egg, banana and nut vendors. The general effect was that of a deserted, flare-lit airport runway.

*

I woke the next day in good health for once and feeling supremely confident. India was becoming a positive pleasure!

And as if to match my mood, the 9am bus tour out to Puri and Konark was the best I'd ever been on. The coach was clean and comfortable, the guide was both pleasant and coherent, and I even found someone to share the day with. This was Norbert, a quirky young German medical student. He reminded me of Kevin.

The first sign that Norbert might be a surrogate Kevin came when he showed me the 16 mosquito bites on his left elbow. 'I do not understand,' he said, his thin black moustache twitching with puzzlement. 'But everything in this country attack me – the dogs bark at me, the holy men shout at me, the monkeys steal from my bag, and the mosquitoes think I am walking lunch.' I laughed. 'I have a friend like that. Do you perhaps have a brother you don't know about living in Lowestoft?'

Bussing it down to Konark, I made a mental note to tackle this stretch of road by cycle next time – mile upon mile of lush, green rice paddy fields and violet water-hyacinths stretched out before me, interpersed with rustic temples, semi-tropical jungles and lively farming villages. 'Spring soon come,' our guide nodded approvingly. 'Number one time to see our countryside.'

Norbert's candidacy to become a second Kevin advanced another step when we came to the famous Sun Temple at Konark. Here, as we surveyed this finest achievement of the mediaeval Orissan sculptors (it was built in the shape of a huge chariot pulled by 7 racing horses to recreate the magnificent progress of the Sun god, Surya, through the heavens) the hapless German attracted the attentions of a bothersome old guide. 'Go away!' said Norbert, but he wouldn't. Instead, the salacious ancient directed us to the erotic panels on the side of the temple and began sucking his teeth and slavering over the more explicit ones. 'This is lesbians, with rats on roof!' he gurgled happily. 'And here is woman giving births – legs akimbo to purify parts over bonfire! Ah, and look at mother swinging her beauties (*breasts) to please father, with young son getting instruction!'

It was all very odd.

But not as odd as our next stop, the holy site of Puri. I saw a resigned look in Norbert's eyes as a large red-bottomed monkey dipped in his bag at the huge Jagannath Temple and made off with his mosquito repellent. 'This is third tube I lose this week,' he complained. 'I think I put a sign on my head that say: "Please rob me."' Poor Norbert. He really should have taken up the offer of a big stick at the foot of the temple to beat off the apes. As it was, he was looking at a matching 16 mosquito bites on his right elbow that night.

But the really odd thing about Puri – something the crooks who had sold us our tickets had neglected to tell us – was that non-Hindus weren't allowed inside the temple. That was why we had had to climb to the roof of the nearby library (and do battle with the monkeys) just to get a peek in. Oh well, we did have a bird's eye view of Puri town from up here, and what a view it was. Even at this 'quiet' time of year, before millions of pilgrims descended on the place for the spectacular Car Festival of June/July, the broad central avenue was a veritable gauntlet of beggars and mendicants, *ganga*-sellers and hawkers, bullock carts and itinerant cows – with scores of dazed Indian families weaving a crazy, erratic path from tour bus to temple.

Norbert's bad luck came to a head as we minded each other's bags while swimming on Puri's famous pilgrimage beach. 'What you *do?'* he announced crossly as a well-aiming local fisherman lassoed him with a heavy rubber ring. 'Here is strong current!' grinned the unapologetic fisherman. 'I save your life!' There was no doubt about it, Norbert had all the makings of a Kevin Mark Two.

Unfortunatedly, as with so many promising encounters this trip, he was heading one way – to Madras – at the end of the tour and I was heading another. In parting, I fished around in my bag and handed him my spare tube of mosquito repellent. He'd be needing it.

Back at the Panthaniwas, I found Mohan waiting for me. He hadn't had a customer all day, so I let him drive me out to the Kalinga Ashok hotel for a good supper. This time the chef got as far as actually cooking it, but then, just as I was tucking in with gusto, there was another power cut and I was left reflecting as to why, when Orissa state was apparently so rich in oil and coal, it spent more time being blacked out than London during the Blitz.

The hotel, plunged into gloom by the electricity failure, was like a tomb. I picked my way through the reception lounge and came across a young American girl reading a book by candlelight. This was Elise, a lively and good natured student over here in India on a journalism scholarship. 'What are you doing here?' she asked me, and when I told her, she laughed. 'India in 66 days? Rather you than me. I've been here a whole month and I feel like I've barely scratched the surface!'

It was another fortuitous encounter. Elise had to leave shortly for her 10.30pm train out to Calcutta. But on this occasion, I was going the same way. I hoped I might run into her there.

Chapter 8

How to Spend Valentine's Day in Calcutta

As agreed, I literally gave Mohan Rao the 'shirt off my back' in return for taking me to the airport the next day. He looked really pleased.

Flying into Calcutta at 8.20pm, I was not so pleased. The cheap airport bus was 'not available at this time', so I flung myself into a positive maelstrom of rickshaw drivers and emerged with one who took me to Sudder Street for 40 rupees. The fact that he charged all the Indians who also piled on board only 25 rupees made me downright displeased. I stood in the lobby of the Fairlawns Hotel, where Elise said she might be staying, and – my stubborn side surfacing in spades – refused to pay more than 30 rupees. Things could have got nasty, but another *shoten zenjin* – a young, sophisticated Indian who turned out to be personnel manager for the Taj Hotel in Delhi – popped up to defuse the situation. 'My name is Soo,' he said as he saw off the stroppy rickshaw driver. 'India can be much trying sometimes – welcome to Calcutta!'

The Fairlawns enjoyed the reputation of being 'the weirdest hotel in India' (several travellers had commented on this) and as I calmed down and checked out the place, I had to agree. A real period piece, with Noel Coward furnishings (flower-patterned drapes and cushions, floral coverlets on the beds etc) and wildly ostentatious lounges, it couldn't be more 'British' if it tried. It also, when I ran into Elise again in the chandeliered lobby, seemed to attract a regular clientele of real oddballs.

'Last night,' she told me, 'I met two missionaires bound for Bhutan, a stranded accountant from Cambridge, a group of video-game smugglers from Sri Lanka, and a Dutchman who'd eaten a drugged *thali* and arrived in Calcutta in just his vest.'

'Is that why the place is so full?' I quizzed her. 'I can't get a single room, I'm having to double up with Soo.'

'I had the same problem,' said Elise, her pert nose twitching with amusement. 'I'm having to double up with a girl called Phoebe. Both of us have been in hysterics since we arrived. The restaurant is full of po-faced waiters in peacock turbans, cummerbunds and white gloves, the twinkling fairy lights over the entrance only go off when a gong sounds for dinner, and the manageress looks and sounds like Barbara Cartland. No wonder travellers hang around here in droves – they're all playing out their parts in a kind of Raj-style soap opera.'

Later on, shortly after Soo went to bed, I got a taste of what she meant. Elise and I settled down in the lobby and were rapidly sucked into a brand-new scene of the ongoing soap. First two French girls, then an Afghani with a limp, then a famous tabla player, and finally a young Englishman who found everything 'fascinating' joined us. The English guy was sipping on his last bit of Johnnie Walker and found the conversation so fascinating that he invited a verbose Calcuttan from another table over to join us. 'I am a *scientist!*' announced the Calcuttan. 'I do not believe in *God!* The universe is expanding and *contracting!*' The tabla player tried to talk about education, but was continually interrupted by the drunken Englishman who said, 'That's *fascinating!*' and 'do you know what *I* think?' Eventually, we narrowed our subjects down to education, materialism and happiness—and began looking around for three props to represent these fundamental concepts. A tube of mosquito repellent became education, a pack of Marlboros stood in for materialism, and 'happiness' found a curious representative in a French-English dictionary. We engaged in animated conversation until two in the morning, and even with these three visual aids being moved back and forth across the table, none of it made any sense at all.

*

I woke early the next morning and, not wanting to disturb Soo, did the sweatiest *gongyo* of my life in the airless, boiling hot toilet of our shared quarters while he slept on in the adjoining bedroom. It was like a sauna.

My overheated prayers resulted in an overheated day. It started out okay, with Elise and me taking a jolly man-powered cart to Mother Theresa's dispensary for the sick in Kalighat. But then Elise's dreams of doing some voluntary work there fell apart. Mother Theresa was too sick to see her.

As bad turned to worse, I returned to the Fairlawns to find Soo checking out. Which meant I had to stump up Rs600 – way over my budget – for another night's stay. I tackled the vague, otherworldly manageress, Mrs Smith, about a possible discount but she was off with the fairies – probably thinking of one of the private video shows she watched upstairs in the evenings. 'Oh no, dear,' she said at last, her pink Barbara Cartland face-pack crinkling with disapproval. 'We can't make *exceptions.*'

Well, I took exception to that and in my mind promised her an equally disapproving report on her hotel. It wasn't just the stuffy, overpriced rooms that got to me or even the weird food (fish fingers for starters?). It was the snotty, unwelcoming, sometimes downright rude staff. They just didn't seem to give a toss about their guests.

But then, having checked out, I found I couldn't find a room elsewhere. I tried the cheap Paragon and Modern lodges, then the Astoria and the Red Shield, but all were full to the brim…with waiting lists. 'At this time of year,' one traveller informed me, 'everybody is gathering like flies in Calcutta for the "big push" up from the hot plains to Darjeeling and Nepal.'

Fortunately, I had the Dutch girl Phoebe in tow (Elise's friend) and she offered me sleeping space on the room of their floor. How kind. I asked Elise if she minded and she said, 'Of course not. It's usually us single girls who have problems getting digs in India. There's a lot of misunderstanding about Western women – landlords often face a moral dilemma as whether to put us up or not. So when we actually get somewhere to stay with no hassle attached to it we're pleased to share!'

At this point, things began to pick up. There was rather a despondent exhibition of local paintings at Calcutta's Birla Art Gallery – titles like 'Grey Landscape', 'Winter is Coming', 'After the Disaster', 'Frightened Nature' and 'Toilet' did not project a happy future for Indian art – but all the paintings were well lit, catalogued and presented. It was also nice and cool in there, a happy escape from the heat and humidity outside.

Later on, all three of us – Phoebe, Elise and me – visited the Oberoi Grand, stuck away in some hard-to-find shopping arcade in the busiest, noisiest part of town. I guess I could have introduced myself and got a free stay at this definitive Raj-style hotel of India (it was a virtual museum of pre-war splendour) but once again I was enjoying my newly found Western company too much to want to give it up. Besides, I wasn't here for the hotel. I was here for its nightly 'Dances of India' programme which was apparently the only entertainment (apart from Mrs Smith's videos) in town. And despite 22 people being crammed into a tiny room to watch it, it was an excellent show. I particularly enjoyed the sitar player who went into a private trance and woke up 20 minutes later after an inspired rendition.

Back at the Fairlawns, after being asked repeatedly by the staff, 'Are you resident here?' I crept silently into Phoebe and Elise's conveniently detached bungalow and got the best sleep in weeks on their floor – a solid eight hours.

*

When I woke up, it was February 14th – Valentine's Day. 'Thanks, Frank!' chorused the girls as our grimy, bumpy morning tour bus hurtled out into the maelstrom of Calcutta's peak-time traffic. 'You could have got us chocolates!'

I felt bad about dragging them along. I also felt bad about the poor bus guide who broke into tears when I said I couldn't understand a word he was saying. He was trying so hard to show off his good English, but what chance did he have? A malfunction on the microphone made his spiel incomprehensible and then we got to Howrah Bridge and he was drowned out completely by the most horrendous din I'd ever heard. Two million people crossed this bridge daily and as we waited our turn, a tidal wave of human and motorised traffic – accompanied by blaring horns, tortured wedding music, and urgently tinkling bicycle bells – washed over and around the bus. 'If this doesn't tell you what Calcutta is all about, nothing will!' I hollered to the girls. But they didn't hear me.

The tour finished at noon, and the girls staggered off it with their fingers still in their ears. 'I'll look out a new room for us, Frank,' said Elise ruefully. 'But you owe me a beer. Those air horns and that bus crashing over pitted, bumpy roads made for the most nerve-wracking, deafening experience of my life!'

For me, the few sights we'd seen – a four-minute glimpse of the world's oldest banyan tree at the Botanical Gardens, then a succession of increasingly uninteresting temples – had been quite secondary to the incredible street life we had seen out of the bus windows. Calcutta, especially around Howrah, was like a giant honey-pot with drones of hungry, busy bees buzzing around it.

In my mind, I finally – after 22 days in India – began composing my first real piece of writing for Paula:

'Despite its notoriety, Calcutta comes as a pleasant surprise to many foreigners. Americans seem to enjoy it because it reminds them of New York – big, brash and action-packed. Australians tend to hate it for the same reasons. Full of holy men, gurus and street temples, Calcutta has been called the soul of India, but it is also her conscience. Here are gathered India's finest artists and musicians, scholars and poets, and her most desperate, poverty-stricken slums. The contrasts between rich and poor, educated and ignorant, old and new, are here more stark and discordant than in any other Indian metropolis. The grand old monuments of the Raj – the Victoria Memorial, the High Court, even the Writers' Building – tower in frightening relief above a grey backdrop of shanty-towns and shattered pavements. Crumbling Georgian mansions look over narrow, festering bazaars. Dust-red London buses crawl alongside hand-drawn rickshaw carts through teeming highways. Busy coffee houses, buzzing with

sophisticated literary debate, look out onto streets littered with uneducated poor. And just down the road from modern Chowringhee, with its glittering Western-style houses and shopping arcades, there is primitive Kalighat with its filth, ordure and animal sacrifices. Calcutta is the distillation – good and bad – of India, and no visit to the country is complete without it.'

I felt good about that report. It came to 811 words, and when I carefully transcribed it into an aerogramme to Paula later on, even I could read it. It was 811 words off the 80,000 words I had been commissioned to write, and the guilt and hopelessness of my near impossible task was reduced by one per cent. Many more reports would have to follow, I inwardly determined. Otherwise, I was looking at the publishing equivalent of a firing squad back home.

By the time I got off my second city bus tour, the afternoon one, I was finished. I was so finished that when I tottered off to the Birla Planetarium to take in its 'English programme' I fell asleep during the show. It was so nice and *cool* in there, and the commentator had such a relaxing, soothing voice. I woke up an hour or so later to hear that I had just missed a demonstration on the passing of Halley's Comet.

Back at the Fairlawns, I found Elise waiting for me – her dust-streaked brown hair combed out and wearing a very practical green sleeveless dress. 'Phoebe just left for Nepal,' she said as she handed me my bag. 'And I just got us nice, cheap digs down the road at the Astoria.'

She had indeed found a very nice room, but neither of us spent much time in it. Elise disappeared off somewhere while I was in the shower and I felt forced out into the streets again to complete my report for Paula. During this stroll, I noted food ration shops for the poor next door to plush jewellery shops, pigs rolling in the gutter outside luxury restaurants, women working hand pumps over open sewers (casually observed by a wealthy businessman urinating on a taxi) and uniformed rich school kids filing down one side of the road while on the other side of a gate lay ragged urchins living on the bottom, bottom line. The word 'contrasts' did not begin to describe these scenes, and the pity which had stirred in my heart in Bombay was as nothing at what I was coming to feel about Calcutta. If I wasn't so selfish, I admonished myself, I'd be doing something to help out here instead of just writing about it.

But what?

It was in a melancholy mood that I arrived at the trendy Blue Sky Café in Sudder St ('THE ONLY CAFÉ FOR YOU KIND OF PEOPLE') and was immediately set upon by a wide-eyed American who wanted to tell me his experience at the Writers' Building. 'It was classic India, man!' he brayed enthusiastically. 'I went for a Sunderbans Tiger Reserve permit and was told to apply to the "rosy-coloured" boy upstairs. This turned out to be a middle-aged man wearing a rose-coloured *shirt.* He was sitting at his table, snowed under by papers, staring up at the ceiling in a mystic trance. So was everybody else. The building was full of people doing absolutely nothing or just reading newspapers. It was real weird!'

But if I had a less than inspiring evening, Elise had it really tough. She got in very late, having been driven down to some obscure temple at the other side of town by a deaf, obstreperous taxi driver whose harangues eventually reduced her to tears. Then things turned round for her. She made it to the modern dance exhibition being put on by her American friends in Park Street and was invited to join Calcutta's famous Saturday Club. This club – geared to the young jet-set elite – entitled her to free swimming, golf, billiards, even free accommodation. 'Ha, ha,' I joshed her with more than a degree of envy in my voice. 'Small chance of you working with Mother Teresa now!'

Elise's luck was most definitely in. The next day, a smartly dressed Indian girl arrived at 9.30am to whisk her off to 'high society' in the Saturday Club. 'I'm sorry, Frank, I might not see you again,' she apologised as she was bundled into the waiting cab. 'But hey, it's been fun. Let's keep in touch!'

It was with a sigh that I watched yet another new friend disappear from my life. But it went with the territory. A large part of me was looking forward to getting off this whistle-stop series of domestic flights around India – I barely had time to say 'Hello' to people before I had to say 'goodbye' again.

Chapter 9

Dark Dealings in Darjeeling

Having flown 300 miles north from Calcutta to Bagdogra, I took a slow 4-hour bus up to Darjeeling and dismounted with some trepidation. I had just learnt that the Youth Hostel – where Megan said she might be if she made it to Darjeeling – was a long 15 minute hike up a virtual mountainside.

As I stood there considering my situation, a fat, cheerful, slant-eyed woman bustled out of her shop beside the bus stop and said, 'You are Frank! I am Ama! Your Scottish friend is here! You come!' I duly followed on, and five minutes later found myself sitting in the homely Shamrock Lodge and happily reunited with Megan.

'You took your time,' observed my cheeky young friend. 'We've been waiting for you for days.'

'How on earth did "Ama" know me?' I said, giving her a happy hug. 'It was pitch dark out there.'

'Oh, that's easy,' said Megan impishly. 'I told her to look out for a guy with glasses.'

'Is that it?' I cocked a disbelieving eye at her. 'You could have at least thrown in the beard!'

Shivering with cold – I was still wearing the same thin jacket I'd worn in Calcutta – I gratefully accepted a bowl of steaming hot noodles and began talking to a Japanese guest about Buddhism. Then I discovered that the whole family, 'Ama' included, chanted Nam-Myoho-Renge-Kyo! They belonged to the Nichiren Shu sect, except for one daughter (in

Delhi) who was Soka Gakkai, the same as me.

The family were interesting. The attractive other daughter, Linda, was apparently the best singer in Darjeeling. Her trendy younger brother, Wong Fu, was an ex-alcoholic rock singer who joined her in a couple of very pleasant songs. As for Ama (real name Mrs Ongel) she reminded me of Old Mary from *South Pacific* – that same kind of warm honesty and inner peace. She told me how beautiful she found *nam-myoho-renge-kyo.* 'I chanting for hour and hour,' she said with a broad smile. 'Never want to stop!'

It was two hours later before I got my room – the best one in the house, with pinewood rafters and a magical view of Mount Kanchenjunga – and even then I had to eat another bowl of noodles ('Eat while hot, no talk!' commanded Ama) before I finally got round to talking to Megan. Like me, she felt that she had somehow 'come home' in Darjeeling – hard to explain, but we both felt that it was *our* kind of place. Unlike me, however, she had been surrounded by Japanese monks and

Buddhists since we had parted ways in Bombay. 'I've even been chanting to catch various trains,' she told me with a twinkle in her eye. 'People have been thinking me mad!'

There was only one problem with Ama's lodge. It was *freezing* and the chest cold I'd caught on the bus up had turned serious. The only hot water available came from a live electric element which the family occasionally threw into large buckets of cold water – novel, but dangerous. I slept that night under a positive mountain of coverlets and blankets.

*

The next day was full of surprises. The first surprise, discounting the fact that it was a Sunday and everything, including the tourist office, was closed, was the layout of Darjeeling. A bustling, widely-dispersed complex of steep steps, deep declines, heaped buildings and winding streets, it was strung out over a wide ridge like a flattened, many-tiered wedding cake. 'It takes days to figure out,' said Megan as we set off up the main drag, Laden-La Rd. 'Everywhere in Darjeeling is a long way up or a long way down. But don't worry, Frank, the scenery will take your mind off the slog!'

She was right about the scenery. All around was dense greenery – not so much the tea plantations for which Darjeeling was famous (they were mainly off the beaten track) but pine forests, mountain meadows, and wildly flowering shrubbery. No wonder the British Raj had seized upon it as a cool summer retreat from the muggy monsoon months of Calcutta.

They were also, Megan informed me, responsible for the hordes of Indians who had descended upon the place. For on each level of the 'wedding cake' there were literally dozens of upmarket public schools where well-to-do Indian children were receiving a 'proper English education'. In this queer quest for Western-style knowledge, they were progressing from kindergartens like 'Mini Land' and 'Love Bud' to impressively-named academies like 'Westpoint' and 'Lorettos'.

Apart from the Indians who were on holiday or visiting their children at school, I didn't think I had seen such a potpourri of racial groups and types in my life. Alongside Tibetan *lamas* in their yellow robes and Tibetan ladies in striped aprons and brocades, there were Gurung farmers from central Nepal, Gurkhas from eastern Nepal, fair-skinned Lepchas and Bhutias from Sikkim, Drukpas from Bhutan, Sherpas from the mountains, and all manner of foreign and domestic tourists. Only in Kathmandu, where I had been with Kevin last year, had I come across anything like such a diversity of cultures and peoples.

'Let's go up to Tiger Hill,' said Megan impulsively. 'This is the first clear weather we've had in days. The dawn views over Mount Kanchenjunga should be spectacular!'

Dawn views? I didn't like the sound of that. 'What time will we have to get up? And where will we stay tonight?'

'Oh, about 4am,' came her careless reply. 'And I hear there's a Tourist Lodge nearby in Ghoom. Let's try and reserve a room.'

I was a bit concerned when a phone call to the lodge elicited no reply. I was even more concerned when Megan bundled me onto a dusty jeep crammed with 19 other people, one crate of eggs and a second crate of rare orchids in the front seat. 'What have you got me into?' I hissed at her. 'There's a chicken pecking at one of my toes and I can't move an inch to do a thing about it!'

Then my concern gave way to relief. Off the bus 30 minutes later, we climbed a mountain ridge affording magnificent views of the valleys below (decorated with conifers, rhododendrons and magnolia) and arrived at Ghoom's tourist lodge to find ourselves the only guests there.

'Talk about luck!' I exclaimed, mopping the sweat from my brow. 'We've got the whole place to ourselves. And wow, check out the view!'

The rustic, wooden lodge was indeed in a beautiful spot, perched on a high plateau overlooking the Kanchenjunga mountain. And we got the best room too, for a ridiculously cheap 15 rupees each. There was however one problem – it was, even before the sun went down, absolutely *freezing*. And since there was a power cut, even the single-bar heater we had was out. We quickly put on every available scrap of clothing and sat on the lodge forecourt, drinking Darjeeling tea, writing postcards through numbed fingers, and watching the lodge staff demolish part of the building. Then, as a howling wind drove us indoors, we prepared, absurdly early, for bed.

It was at this point that I sensed trouble. I felt something coming, and chanted about it. The trouble was that, all of a sudden, my feelings towards Megan – which to date had been completely platonic – had, since reaching Darjeeling, been changing. I was beginning to really fancy her. And our conversation that evening, after all the jolly jokes and laughter were over, had been drifting inexorably towards relationships. Most pertinent of all, it was so dreadfully cold in that room and we only had one double bed to sleep in. I did *gongyo*, and chanted that only if it was right for our happiness would what I sensed might happen actually come to pass.

Well, it did. It was all extremely strange, but at the same time perfectly natural. In retrospect, it seemed almost destined that – with all the strange meetings we'd been having – Megan and I would end up getting involved. Especially since we took such pleasure and happiness in each other's company. 'Do you mind if we cuddle up for a bit?' I ventured hesitantly. 'My teeth are chattering like a crazed monkey!' Megan's big-eyed, boyish features creased in a broad grin. 'I don't mind at all,' she said. 'Just don't cough in my ear.'

We were 'engaged' from 8pm to midnight – one way of spending a dull evening at Ghoom – and then I head-butted Megan in the dark and nearly knocked her out. And it wasn't just her that was feeling shell-shocked. I hadn't been expecting this at all. 'Here we go again,' I thought as I hacked and wheezed right through the night. 'Just like with Anna, I've commenced a relationship in just about the worst physical condition possible.'

My mind in a whir, I hardly slept a wink.

*

The sunrise at Tiger Hill was breathtaking. Having risen at 4am and made the stiff, steep ascent up to the viewing point (we arrived toasty warm, all the Indians who turned up in buses and jeeps were frozen solid) we were rewarded with the clearest, most wonderful mountain views we had ever seen. The massive peak of Kanchenjunga reared up, surrounded by Markala, Lhotse and several other summits. To the far left, the central of three peaks, was Everest. 'So, it was worth it,' I murmured to Megan. 'Yes,' she replied, equally impressed. 'And would you believe it, I left my camera back at the lodge.'

Returning back down, we next visited Ghoom Monastery – the oldest and most famous monastery in Darjeeling. Established in 1850 by a famous Mongolian astrologer-monk, it belonged to the 'Yellow Sect' and housed a massive image of Maitreya, the 'Buddha to Come'. Walking inside this dark, tomb-like structure, all the hairs stood up on the back of my neck. It was just like a set from *The Inn of the Sixth Happiness* – authentically Tibetan in every respect. Ranged around the large seated Buddha were gongs, drums, neat stacks of prayer stools for the monks, and a large raised dais for the head of the order. The air was thick and musty, a single beam of light penetrated the gloom from a small ceiling skylight, and all was silent. 'Wow,' muttered Megan respectfully. 'This is the nearest thing to Tibet you'll see without actually going there.'

Very tired now, we walked back to Ghoom railway station – with its amusing signs like DON'T BE AFRAID OF UNNECESSARILY and KEEP A STRICT WATCH AROUND YOURSELF – and caught the 9.30am train back to Darjeeling. It was a lovely ride, the little 'toy-train' giving me a taster of what I had missed by taking the bus up here from Bagdogra instead of the (much) slower train from New Jalpaiguri.

Back at Shamrock Lodge, we moved into a huge 4-bedded room where I kept banging my head on the low ceilings. 'You're a complete mess, Frank,' Megan gently scolded me. 'Why don't you get your head down and sleep for a bit?' But sleep was impossible. The primary 'Mini School' next door were making a right old racket (the kids howling 'Baa Baa, Black Sheep' at the top of their voices) and Ama's oldest son was demolishing a ground floor room. 'Don't worry about me,' I winced as I poured a bucket of electrolysed water over my head. 'All I need is a shower.'

What I really needed was a stretcher. As I shambled out like a zombie to 'see Darjeeling', my eyes were streaming, my lungs were red-raw, and my legs had turned to water.

Somehow, I made it to the Bengali Natural History Museum (where Megan went into raptures over some Nepali fish she recognised) and then to the tourist office where a helpful lady gave me all the information I needed in 20 minutes. But that was about it. 'We'd better get you home,' Megan said at last, and dragged me – via picturesque back streets full of smiley, happily waving locals – back to the Shamrock.

Making love again was out of the question. Not only had I reached a point of total physical exhaustion, but Megan had eaten something which hadn't agreed with her and was suffering from a bad tummy ache. Added to which, both of us were finding the transition from friends to lovers very unsettling – we kept forgetting that it had happened!

'How do we get any consistency into this thing?' I asked through a particularly violent coughing fit. 'Two days in Pokhara, two days in Delhi, and six days in Rajasthan last year, now six days in Bombay and three days in Darjeeling. What next?'

Megan rolled her warm, brown eyes at me. 'What indeed?' she said.

Lingering in the background, of course, was my on-off relationship with Anna back home in the U.K. I had written her twice since leaving a month ago and hadn't received a word in return. Had she fallen out of love with me? Had she finally come to her senses and realised that a long-term relationship with an itinerant travel writer was never going to be a good idea?

I was so confused.

Chapter 10

Bad Bus to Bagdogra

'I really shouldn't be travelling today,' I told Megan as I hauled myself aboard the 10am bus back to Bagdogra. 'Mars is opposing the Sun in my horoscope.'

A look of mixed concern and amusement crossed my young friend's features. 'I know you have to be in Delhi tonight,' she said, giving me a parting hug. 'But really, Frank, you're the most superstitious bloke I know. Can't you challenge this with your chanting?'

To be fair, I had chanted about it but couldn't overcome the feeling of impending doom. Plus I was in a catatonic coma as I slumped into my prime seat right at the front of the bus alongside the driver. The only thing that perked my mood up was the scenery on the way down – it was *beautiful*. But then, as my eyes drank in the cool mountain valleys all aglow with early-Spring flowering shrubbery, I noticed the cautionary road signs dotted along the highway. IF YOU WANT TO SEE THE HEAVEN, DRIVE SLOW, IF YOU WANT TO SEE THE HELL, DRIVE FAST said one. IT IS BETTER TO BE THE GOOD MR MOTORIST THAN TO BE THE LATE MR MOTORIST said another. 'Blimey,' I muttered to myself. 'Is it really that unsafe up here?'

Moments later, I had my answer. As we rounded one of the numerous knife-edge bends winding down to Bagdogra, a puff of dust about 100 yards ahead cleared to reveal a jeep coming the other way. And it was hurtling towards us at top speed.

'Ram-Ram, Ram-Ram,' murmured our driver, giving the little plastic god above his head a lucky shake. 'Nam-myoho-renge-kyo, Nam-myoho-renge-kyo,' I mumbled in return. Then, as the jeep showed no sign of slowing down, the driver took a quick, urgent look at me and I took a quick, urgent look at him, and we pulled all the stops out. *'Ram-Ram, Ram-Ram, RAM-RAM!'* he bellowed, tugging the little plastic god so hard that it came away in his hand. *'Nam-myoho-renge-kyo, NAM-MYOHO-RENGE-KYO!'* I screeched back at him.

Everything happened in slow motion. A silent scream filled the back of my throat as the jeep slammed into us head on. Then our bus teetered dangerously on the edge of a 2000 foot drop. Then, with a terrifying squeal of tyres and brakes, it righted itself and we all began to breath again. The miracle was – and here I had to admit the superiority of Buddhism over astrology – that although the jeep was a complete write-off, all four of the inebriated Indian partygoers in it emerged unscathed. And our bus was able to proceed – with only superficial damage – on to Bagdogra.

The big plan, when I flew into Delhi at 6.20pm, was to grab my first free stay at an Oberoi hotel – this time, I had no Jessica or Elise to hold me back from a bit of 5-star luxury. But once again, I was thwarted. 'I am so sorry,' apologised the manager at the plush Oberoi Maidens hotel in Sham Nath Marg. 'But we think you are coming *next* month. Look, see, here is the letter from your publisher. You are not expected until *March* 18th. We now have full occupancy!' I stared at the letter from Paula in disbelief. It did indeed say March, not February. How could she have been so incompetent?

My fallback – given that Delhi had a dearth of mid-range hotels and I couldn't afford them anyway – was the budget Hotel Chanakya in downtown Paharganj. I had stayed here with Kevin last year and had done battle with cockroaches, gecko lizards, a *faux* laundry boy who nicked all my clothes, and a ceiling fan with only two speeds – ultra-slow and turbo-speed fast. The latter mode had plucked a gecko off the wall and blown it clear across my room.

This time I didn't even *get* a room. The whole of Delhi was packed out (it was the peak tourist season) and I had to flash all my press credentials to even get a dormitory bed. And then the rowdy Bombay transport officials who occupied the rest of the dorm forced me onto the street again. They looked like just the type to chat all through the night. I ended up grabbing just three hours of sleep on a dark piece of floor at Delhi airport – a towel under my head and my head on my bag to prevent theft. 'I'm a travel writer,' I thought to myself grimly. 'Not a dosser!' But at least I was warm and safe – unlike the thousands of people I knew who would be sleeping on the pavements that night.

Chapter 11

Pony Treks and Toboggans

The next day marked the end of the 3-week air ticket which had carried me three-quarters round the continent of India. I had to pinch myself that it had gone so fast…and so smoothly. And Steve said it couldn't be done, that something was bound to happen to trip me up. I laughed at Steve in my mind. But then I remembered how many near-trips and narrow escapes I had had. There was definitely an angel on my shoulder!

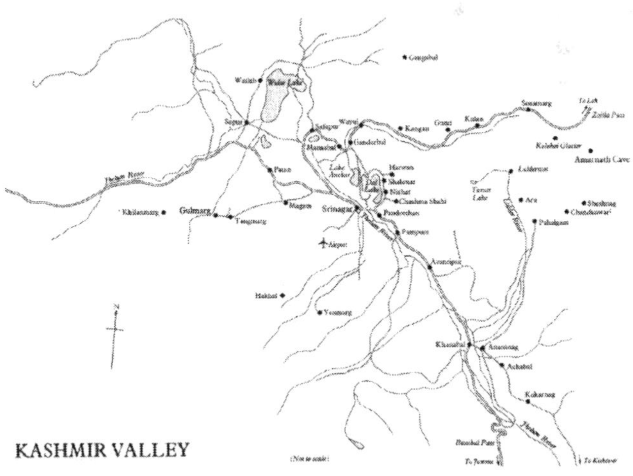

KASHMIR VALLEY

The 6.30am flight up to Srinagar was a treat, particularly the last half hour of it. Gliding over a mirage range of rolling, snow-capped mountains – the clouds hanging motionless over their peaks like balls of fluffy cotton wool – the city suddenly burst into view: a bright gem glittering in a valley of green meadows, rivers and lakes.

'Who has not heard of the Vale of Cashmere?' suggests the poet. The Moghul emperors certainly had – each one that left this cool valley of mountain charm to go empire-founding forever dreamt of going back. But then none of them, I suspected, had arrived in its summer capital, Srinagar, after its worst winter in 23 years. Driving into town along wide avenues of tall *chinars* (oriental plane trees) I was surprised, and more than a little disappointed, to find how wet, grey and chilly it all was. The people were well wrapped up in blankets and woolly hats, and on both sides of the road, the rice paddy fields were flooded.

At the small Poste Restante near the Government Arts Emporium I found just one letter waiting for me. It was from Anna. Pocketing it for later perusal, I proceeded straight on to Srinagar's famous Dal Lake, where hundreds of houseboats of all sizes, shapes and categories were moored. Most of them looked dirty and grubby on the outside – I later learnt things had been so bad lately (tourists staying away in droves due to political problems and bad weather) that few houseboat owners had been able to afford renovation or upkeep of their boats. Things *must* have been bad, because the first boat I was shown – the Pasdona – was a real deluxe job complete with rich furnishings, antique cupboards, exotic carpets and wood panelling throughout. 'Good Lord,' I thought as I negotiated a ridiculously cheap Rs60 day rate, including breakfast. 'This is a massive step up from the little cell-like rooms I've been used to in India proper!' Though I did have some misgivings. There was no light bulb in the bedroom, no toilet flush, and no lock on the door. Well, they had the lock, but not the key!

Gingerly crossing over the marsh outside the boat via a

narrow plank, I visited the amazing Tourist Reception Centre (the largest tourist complex in Asia) and learnt the history of the houseboats. They had come into being during the British Raj, apparently, when the Dogra Maharajahs of Kashmir (who had gained sovereignty of Kashmir in 1846) forbade the British to build or own land here. Undismayed, the British officers took to the lake instead, living on the waters of the Dal in fully equipped, beautifully ornate, houseboats. From the first one constructed in 1876, there were now more than 1300 houseboats on Srinagar's lakes.

My curiosity satisfied, I next decided to satisfy my stomach. A short walk from the tourist centre took me to the friendly Moghul Durbar restaurant on Residency Rd which Elise had told me served up the most authentic Kashmiri food in Srinagar. She was right. My appetite having increased in leaps and bounds since meeting Megan again, I absolutely gorged myself on Kashmiri naan (fruit-topped naan bread), *tabaq-mazh* (grilled spare ribs cooked in cashew-nut, poppyseed, and onions) and the traditional meatballs cooked in savoury curd dish known as *guzhtaba.*

Then, as I sat back, sated, I suddenly remembered the letter from Anna. 'Oh, how nice of her to write at last,' I thought. 'I wonder how she's getting on.'

Then I opened up the thin, blue aerogramme and my wonder turned to horror.

My dear lovely Frank it said. *How are you? Wish you could answer. I'm experiencing the absence makes the heart grow fonder syndrome and get this crying lump every time I chant for you. I HAVE FORGOTTEN ALL THE THINGS THAT IRRITATE ME ABOUT YOU! Look, guess what, I'M COMING OUT TO INDIA TO SEE YOU! I'm arriving in New Delhi on 2nd March and staying for A WHOLE MONTH! Why am I coming? Seems strange to be doing this in some ways but I do feel that I need the perspective and I would like to be of some use with the book. They'll be two pairs of eyes etc for at least some of the trip. SEE YOU IN DELHI!!! Lots of love and kisses, Anna xxxx*

I rubbed my eyes in disbelief. Anna was coming to India? And for a whole month? What had prompted such a change of heart in her? She had been less than enthusiastic about me taking on this guidebook – now she wanted to come over and help me write it? My mind racing, I scrolled back to the warm and welcoming letter I had written her back in Bombay. 'This is such a beautiful country,' I had enthused. 'I wish you could come see it for yourself!' Had she really interpreted this as an open invitation?

I was torn. Part of me really did want to see Anna again. She had always had a large place in my heart and it would be lovely to be able to share India with her. But another part of me remained stubbornly independent. I had become used to my own company now and couldn't see how she could fit in with the busy, intense schedule I had set for myself – upping sticks and moving from one place to another each day, interviewing people left, right and centre.

Then, almost as an afterthought, I turned the letter over and found myself even more gobsmacked. *I hope you're in Kashmir now,* said the neatly typed postscript. *I had this incredibly jealous feeling the other day that you might have decided to travel with Megan and fall for her. I felt it very strongly but that didn't concern me as much as my hopes for your health and safety. Take care, Frank!*

This second bombshell was even more difficult to deal with than the first. How could Anna have known about me and Megan possibly hooking up? Even *we* didn't see it coming!

God, I wished I had received this letter a week ago. Life would have been so much simpler.

Then something happened to take my mind off the whole business. 'Sir! Sir!' said the grizzled old Muslim who tackled me outside the restaurant. 'My name Gulam Mohammed! I have very nice houseboat! You look!' White bearded, leathery-faced, and wearing a woollen shepherd's cap he looked like a troll out of *The Lord of the Rings*. 'Oh, alright then,' I said, secretly welcoming the distraction. 'But I have to warn you, I already have a houseboat.'

Gulam's boat – the New Chattri Palace – wasn't half as swish or clean as the Pasdona but it was much closer to what 'action' Srinagar had to offer. Also, and here I had to applaud the cunning rogue's guile, he sweetened my decision with a cup of special cinnamon tea for my bad chest. 'Does Sir want half-sugar or full-sugar?' he crooned solicitously. 'One lump or two?'

I grinned to myself. Old Gulam promised to be a real character. And when he offered me the whole boat for Rs70 a day, including all meals and his undivided attentions as personal guide round Srinagar, I was sold. 'Sir will have first-class experience,' he assured me with a determined glint in his eye. 'Sir will be one of the family!'

*

I woke at 6am after a much-needed ten hours sleep and tried to sneak off the Pasdona unnoticed. But it wasn't easy. First, the *khansamah* (cook boy) arrived with a very tempting breakfast of heavily-buttered Kashmiri bread, two boiled eggs, and pot of tea. Then the old boy who owned the boat turned up with a brand-new light bulb. 'Sorry, you're too late,' I mumbled with some embarrassment. 'Last night, I nearly break leg looking for toilet.'

The walk over to Gulam's boat from the Pasdona was sheer poetry: the morning mist hung like a shroud over mirror-calm waterways, the stillness of the lake was broken only by the occasional rhythmic paddle of a gondola-like *shikara* coming up the sleepy backwater, and the ghostly, grey hulks of houseboats jutted out from the silent jetty like dormant crocodiles. Then came the dawn and I stood on a rickety old wood bridge and watched the soaring mountain backdrop – a stately line of snow-capped peaks – glow rose-pink by the light of the morning sun.

'Hello, Sir!' said Gulam upon my arrival. 'Welcome to my humble palace!' He had a big grin on his weathered face and his arms were flapping an empty, handless welcome from within a long, thick woollen poncho. I eyed that poncho with envy. If anything, Srinagar was even colder than Darjeeling. 'Sir must have my *pheran*!' insisted my gracious host. 'Can put fire inside also!'

Fire inside? What was he talking about? Oh yes, I'd heard of those little fire-pot braziers which locals carried around inside their thick winter garments. I accepted the poncho with gratitude but declined the second proposition with a polite wave of the hand. My assets may have been frozen, but I didn't fancy setting fire to them.

Gulam's poncho acted like an invisibility cloak. As soon as he shuttled me back into town in his little *shikara*, I suddenly shed my tourist identity and melted into the local populace. So invisible did I become indeed that I managed to reach the tourist office with not one tout offering me tea, houseboats, silk, hashish or a visit to a crafts emporium.

The day was set aside for a trip to Pahalgam, a popular holiday resort 96 kilometres east of Srinagar. The four hour outward bus journey made some interesting stops (including an ashram where a street doctor offered to cure my cold by applications of leeches) and the scenery spoke for itself – a glorious vista of majestic mountains, green pine forests, and meadows of bright yellow saffron.

Coming into Pahalgam, lines of bearded, weather-worn, *hookah*-smoking shepherds appeared at the roadside and gangs of local youths leapt onto the side of our bus for a free ride into town. It seemed to be their favourite sport. Hunger struck at this point and I invaded the Hotel Apsara near the bus stop for a short repast. Bypassing MUTTON CHAMPS and POISON COFFEE, PER CUP on the menu, I opted instead for a cheap vegetarian meal. Then I noticed the enigmatic sign on the toilet door: DO NOT PUT DUST IN BATH. I went inside and found no bath or tub or even a toilet bowl. Instead, there was just a hole in the ground…and a 20 foot drop into the snow if you missed your footing.

The big thing to do in Pahalgam was a pony trek, but I wasn't planning on one. I had been seriously traumatised in the equine department by an experience I had had on a Club Continental 18 to 30s holiday in Ibiza a few years earlier. No sooner had I got off the plane than the club reps shoved a bottle of green alcohol with a worm in it down my throat. Then they had pushed me on a donkey, along with about a dozen other inebriated guests, and made us race against each other. Those poor donkeys. They went off in all directions as they tried to dislodge us (one guy ended up in a tree) and I only won by complete accident – one finger on the donkey's back while the rest of me dragged along the ground under it.

'Hey mister!' shouted up the gap-toothed young ragamuffin who'd spotted me exiting the toilet. 'Pony for you?' I declined with a polite nod of the head, but he was insistent. 'This number one pony! You like!' I took a long, hard look at the short, shaggy-haired animal. It didn't look big enough to take a child, let alone a fully grown man. 'Okay,' I sighed. 'But shouldn't it be me taking it for a walk instead of the other way round?'

I needn't have worried. The pony was both strong and amazingly sure footed. Which it had to be since the winter snows were just melting and the narrow trails were full of treacherous, muddy inclines and declines. I did the hour-long Four Points trek which took me out to the four points of optimum beauty overlooking the valley. Riding along conifer-lined mountain paths and over shallow rushing streams of leaping trout, I came at last to the higher ridges, affording superb alpine views. Then, on my return, I got off my pony for a while and met with some local shepherds who let me pick up and hold one of their baby lambs. My faith in the equine community was restored.

It was dark by the time we returned to Srinagar. Here I found Gulam sitting in his *shikara*, waiting for me. 'Sir must be cold!' he said as he ferried me back to the houseboat. 'Hot shower is coming!' Then, even before I was allowed in the shower, he started going on about carpets. 'Sir should have one of our beautiful Kashmir carpets – you make big profit in U.K.!' This I knew to be a lie. According to Megan, who had been here last year, the Kashmir carpet business had been ruined by big businessmen flying to Srinagar and buying up millions of pounds worth of carpets and flooding the market with them back in the West. 'Yes, the Kashmiris *do* make the best handmade carpets in the world,' she had told me. 'But you can now buy them for the same price in London or New York high streets as in Kashmir.'

The more Gulam went on about carpets, the more irritated I got. Then, to cap it all off, he served me up a 'supper' of undercooked chips, overcooked (black) chops, and mushy, greasy tomatoes. The only thing he got right was the bottle of beer I had ordered. But that didn't work out either. Having finally had my shower, I discovered that he had forgotten to supply a bottle opener and I had a fun half hour bouncing it about the boat, vainly trying to open it. 'I must get more chanting in,' I thought as I dismally drifted off to sleep. 'My life state is slipping badly.'

*

One of the fundamental precepts of my Buddhism is 'no complaint', but I woke up next morning with complaint in the kernel of my heart. 'What was with the raw chips last night?' I berated Gulam when he appeared with my breakfast. 'They couldn't have been cooked for more than a minute!' He had an incredible excuse. 'Cooking in *ghee* (*clarified butter) not good for Sir's cold,' he smirked. 'So I cook in oil. *Lightly* cook. Best for Sir's chest!'

'What a load of cod,' I thought, but let him get away with

it. Overall, I was impressed by Gulam's simplicity, honesty and modesty. He said that everything he did was 'written in his hand', so he didn't allow anyone on his boat who dealt in or took drugs. He was also a devout Muslim and spent the whole day cycling around town with me, showing me his favourite mosques. None of them should have allowed me in, as a non-believer, but my woolly cap and 'invisibility' *pheran* opened every door. Indeed, as I fortuitously arrived at the main Hazratbal Mosque for the big Friday pray-in and thousands of Muslims from miles around flocked in, I found myself swept into the main hall and bowing and prostrating myself along with all the faithful. What an experience!

Outside the mosque, I found a real taste of Kashmir: an amazing bazaar complete with grizzled mountain men sucking *hookahs*, women in black purdah haggling expertly over meat and bread, vast cauldrons bubbling with bright-red holy food, street dentists and opticians fitting old dentures and specs onto hopeful passers-by, and lots of dust, smoke and noise.

After moaning to Gulam that he was overcharging me (a 'C' class boat was listed at Rs65 a day, not Rs70) he took me to the Houseboat Association opposite the tourist office to get an up-to-date listing of houseboat tariffs. They didn't have one. Instead, they moaned back at me that corrupt Indian officials were ruining their business. 'The Kashmiris are an isolated people,' Megan's words rang in my ears. 'Yes, they are part of India, but they *feel* much closer to Pakistan. All the recent riots, blockades and curfews have been the result of the Indian government levying steep price increases affecting energy and fuel. Kashmir's problem is that she is dependent on India, and doesn't like it. But the alternative is even worse. Were she to secede from India, she may – and this is the main fear – have the Communists strolling in from China.'

Back on my boat, Gulam tried to justify his five rupee surcharge. 'Sir must have light!' he insisted and tried to improve the lighting in my room by rigging up a complicated wiring pattern which left me with *three* dim bulbs instead of just two. The extra one dangled a foot over my bed, enabling me to crouch right under it and do some writing. How ingenious. Then he went the extra mile and made me an excellent cheese curry with rice. 'This rice is Kashmiri rice – Vitamin B!' he announced proudly. 'Very *tastable* rice!'

After haggling a bit – I wanted Gulam's poncho, he wanted my watch – I retired to bed with a single thought in my head. Where were all the Western tourists? I had not seen one since getting here. Maybe they were hanging out in their cosy, luxurious houseboats waiting for the bitter cold to go away, but I didn't think so. This was my third day in Srinagar and it looked like I was the only Westerner in town. Did this bother me? Not at all. After the rest of India, I was really appreciating the privacy!

*

The next day was earmarked for a relaxing *shikara* ride on Dal Lake, and it was a real experience. Making my way down to Boulevard Rd, I negotiated a 3-hour round trip of the lake with an unusually un-pushy boat-man for just 25 rupees. Then, as I climbed into his low-canopied, exotically decorated *shikara* and sank into one of the plush, silk-cushioned seats, I prepared myself for what Megan had warned me would be the only non-relaxing part of the trip: a sudden, urgent onslaught of floating '*shikara* shops' which ran out at me like an invading armada. 'Blimey, this is like a scene from Hitchcock's *The Birds!'* I thought as first one, then two, then a whole convoy of wildly paddling boats tacked onto mine and drifted down the waterways with me. They were manned by grinning, waving, hallooing traders with unlikely names like 'Tasty Tailor', 'Crocodile'. and 'Nick the Jeweller' (Crocodile's cousin), and they were determined to sell me something, anything. Reeling under the simultaneous assault of kebab-stick men, *papier-mache*-men, carved-knife men, wood-carved-box men, fruit-market men ('You like *apples?'*) and jacket-stole men, I ended up buying a racoon hat, six tolers of red saffron, and three semi-precious stone necklaces. It was a mistake telling them I was a Buddhist: I was instantly inundated with Tibetan prayer-wheels, prayer bells, and little stone Buddhas.

Past all the *shikara* salesmen, I enjoyed a quiet, undisturbed ride up to Nehru Park, where all the five star 'deluxe' houseboats were moored. They bore amusing names like NOAH'S ARK, NEW NEIL ARMSTRONG, KING'S THROWN and (my personal favourite) DONGOLA SUPERDUPER DELUXE WITH WATER SKIZ. *Shikara* gondolas drifted past with honeymooning Indian couples. They had titles like INDIAN DREAM DISCO HA HA, and were followed by young lads propelling small dugga-boats with heart-shaped paddles. These budding entrepreneurs paused briefly to offer Pepsis and choc-ices before continuing on.

Back on my boat, my uncomplaining old *shikara* man took me next to the Floating Gardens – drifting silently through a wonderland of winding water-corridors carpeted with meadow-green lichen and pink-red water lilies. Then he located the 'old market' – a floating bazaar which moved daily – and gladly guided me to the best places for shopping.

Though shopping was no longer really an option. 'Kashmir is turning out expensive,' I thought as the tour came to an end. 'Somehow, I've got through a hundred dollars in just four days.' On the plus side, this part of India was really growing on me. Escaping off the busy river into my quiet houseboat haven was great. 'You just can't do this in India proper,' I told my Walkman after a nice hot shower. 'No escape possible, except in luxury hotels. Sometimes, not even then!'

My last full day in Kashmir opened at 3am when I was woken by all the crockery in the small kitchen behind my bedroom clattering away. This turned out to be Gulam's pet rat 'Billy'. Billy, I learnt, came and ate any dinner leftovers each night. He was particularly fond of curry.

The rest of the day was high adventure. I boarded the 9.30am day tour bus to Gulmarg with considerable anticipation. Situated 53kms from Srinagar, this beautiful mountain resort was famous for its flowers, for its outstanding natural golf course (at 2650 metres, the highest in the world) and for its winter skiing resort. 'In high season, it's packed out,' Megan had told me. 'Busloads of rich Indians roll in every few minutes and are greeted by exultant hordes of pony-men, toboggan-men, ski-instructors and assorted guides. The women go skiing in saris and army boots, the men dress up in strange coats made from acrylic fur, with high collars, gold buttons, and huge plastic elasticated belts.'

But this was not high season. It was about as low season as

it could get. And about two hours out, as we got to Tangmarg (13kms below Gulmarg), we realised we had a problem. The snow started coming down in sheets. Teaming up with the only other two Westerners on the bus – an Irish obstetrician called Anne and a farmer from Kent called Ian – I hid out in the quaint Mahajan Restaurant ('HERE MAKE TEA OR HAVE IMMEDIATE') while a gaggle of touts, pony-men and jeep-men argued the toss over who would see us up to the mountain. In winter, I'd learnt from the tourist centre, the bus rarely went the whole way up – it just dumped folk in Tangmarg and they got a jeep the final leg to Gulmarg. On this occasion, however, the bus *did* attempt it. And got stuck in a snowdrift halfway there. 'Extremely foolhardy,' grumbled Anne as we all got out and walked the final few kilometres up to Gulmarg. 'Yes, well, you've got to see the funny side of it,' I said with a grin. 'Here we are, fighting our way through to the "meadow of flowers" – only to find the whole place buried under seven feet of snow.'

Then, of course, having made it to the top and having had the weakest cup of hot chocolate imaginable in Gulmarg's one and only visible restaurant, we had to think about going down again.

'I'm not walking down,' said Ian, his weathered farmer's face set in a stubborn pout. 'There must be another way.' Then his eyes alighted on the three low wooden sleds the porters had dragged up behind the bus. 'Ah ha,' he crowed, pointing us to them. 'There's our meal ticket!' Anne and I exchanged a look of puzzlement. 'What are they?' we said in unison, and Ian said, 'they're toboggans. Have you never seen a toboggan before?' I considered this and could think of only one. It was called Rosebud and it figured heavily in Orson Welles's film *Citizen Kane.* Rosebud had made little Kane very happy as a child, but was ultimately a symbol of his decline and fall. I eyed the toboggans with suspicion. Did they have the same fate in mind for me?

There followed the most exhilarating 15 minutes of my life. 'What a buzz!' I cried as my sled made a mad, hair-raising 2000ft descent down winding, twisting toboggan runs at incredible speeds. 'Sit! Sit!' screamed my crazed driver whenever we clipped a tree or 'legs up!' when that extra bit of speed was called for. 'Gosh, this looks dangerous!' I remarked at one point, eyeing up a precipice we had stopped at the brink of. 'Oh, that is nothing!' replied the driver airily. 'We pass *really* dangerous part just back!'

Whenever it got too steep to toboggan, we slid down the mountainside on our bums. 'I'm absolutely *soaked!'* complained Anne as Tangmarg came into view. 'I don't care, I'm having a ball!' I laughed in reply. Then I collided with a tree and was completely buried by an avalanche of snow that came down from its pregnant branches.

We waited two more hours for the rest of our bus passengers to pick their way down the mountain on foot and rejoin us, and in all of that time I was steaming. I was in fact steaming so much – as the log fire in Tangmarg's small 'porter' restaurant dried off my sopping-wet poncho – that Ian and Anne couldn't see me. No matter. I got a lot of information from Ian, including where to stay if I ever made it back to Gulmarg again. 'It's called the City View Hotel, and it's just like staying with the Addams family,' he said as he toasted his damp woolly cap over the fire on the end of a ski. 'There's an old cook called Wally who does the best food in Kashmir, an eccentric waiter called Ramone who does his best to be deliberately rude – "What you want, you?" – and a Bruce Lee clone called 'Dragon' who appears every night to tell guests how he wandered round the Himalayas for four years, and how he can take off his clothes with just two fingers.'

I found this funny, but Anne didn't. 'That's what gets me about the Kashmiris,' she said, a further flush coming to her apple-red cheeks. 'Some of them do talk a lot of rot. I went to a travel agency in Srinagar to book this Gulmarg tour, and the manager wasn't having it. He wanted me to go to the Kolahoi Glacier instead. "Is good value!" he chirped annoyingly. "You get good food! You get fresh eggs and live chicken! You get chicken in the basket – flying chicken on the mountain! You get caramel custard – yes, with a cherry! You get banana fritter with honey at height of 16,000 feet! Tourists like that kind of thing, you know?"'

Ian and I laughed. 'What did you tell him?' we asked.

'I told him to shut up about that bloomin' glacier and give me that ticket to Gulmarg. If he didn't, I added, I'd tell him where to stick that cherry.'

After further delays, including a punctured tyre, our rescued bus got back to Srinagar absurdly late, at 8.30pm. ‘Where Sir *go?*’ said Gulam, jumping out of his *shikara* like a frightened rabbit. ‘I think Sir must be *dead!*’ I gave him a quick pinch to show that I wasn’t and then enticed him to paddle me over to my houseboat. Here, and this was really touching, he fussed over me like a mother hen, lighting a glorious wood fire and serving up a piping-hot vegetable *pulao* meal. It was his finest hour, the food was so delicious, but I couldn’t eat it all. In a flourish of magnanimity, I told him to leave the remainder for Billy.

A tear trickled down one of Gulam’s leathery cheeks as I prepared to leave the next morning. He was genuinely sad to see me go. ‘Sir have good time?’ he said miserably. ‘Sir will recommend to friends?’ I assured him that I would and gave him a parting hug. ‘You say you will make me part of family, and you did,’ I said by way of cheering him up. ‘I will pray for you, my friend. You are a good man.’

Chapter 12

Jammed up in Jammu

I boarded the 7.45am bus to Jammu with considerable unease. It would be my first marathon road trip this tour of India – no more quick and easy domestic flights for me. But I needn't have worried. On board was an entertaining Australian called Martin and four hours flew by as he filled me in on places I wouldn't be visiting, like Ladakh and Leh, while in return I talked to him about Buddhism. Then, around 1pm, the bus suddenly ground to a dead halt. 'This ain't good,' said Martin, leaning out of his window. 'Looks like the traffic jam to end all traffic jams.' I stood up and craned over him to look for myself. 'Blimey, you're right,' I said with a whistle. 'There's literally hundreds of vehicles stretching out ahead of us for as far as the eye can see!'

The cause of the hold-up was clear as soon as we stepped off the bus. Even from where we were standing, a mile or so away, vast chunks of mountainside were dropping away and crashing to the ground. It was the first landslide I'd seen outside of a disaster movie.

While waiting for the road to be cleared, I had another little word with my Walkman. 'I would describe the Srinagar/Jammu run as one of the *great* bus journeys of India. Twelve or more hours of stunning scenery, perilous barrier-free mountain tracks, and the nerve-racking, edge-of-your-seat excitement of never knowing if you're going to reach the other end in one piece. The sides of the rocky road are strewn with the hulks of vehicles either recently crashed or recently retrieved from gaping chasms. Every bus or truck on this route drives like the very devil and just to make you feel even less safe, there's a series of astonishing and disconcerting road-signs: "DARLING I WANT YOU, BUT NOT SO FAST", "MY CURVES ARE DANGEROUS, GO ROUND THEM SLOWLY", and (my personal favourite) "I LONG FOR MY LOST LOVE – SPEEDING, HE WENT INTO THE RIVER.""

The first thing that struck me when we finally rolled into Jammu at 10.30pm was that I was back in India proper, with all the heat, dust, sacred cows, and temples. The second thing that struck me was the strong military presence – Jammu was very close to the Pakistan border and tensions were evidently running high. Grabbing just about the only room left in town – a grotty cell in the Hotel Apsara – I moved next door to the Hotel Naz for some late night sustenance. The menu here was a hoot – ESTAMBLE EGG ON TOAST, FRAY EGG and SWEEP CORN SOUP – and so were the waiters. 'Why does my coffee have hot milk, hot water, but no coffee in it?' I asked one of them. 'So sorry, sir,' came the happy reply. 'This is the only item we are serving!'

Jammu did not impress me. Not only were the general populace nervous with so many armed police and soldiers on the streets, but when a sparrow flew into my room and squawked me awake at 6am I couldn't find a restaurant open for breakfast. At the Tourist Home Hotel, a little old man cried, "Wait! Wait! Manager is coming!' But the manager was not coming. He was urinating against a 'Stick no bills' sign on the other side of the road. So I ordered some plain chapatis at the unfriendly *dhaba* next door. And got served a red-hot chilli *paratha* instead. That woke me up.

At 9am, Jammu's tourist office opened its door to me and

revealed itself the most useless in all India. It had no hand-out information on the city, it offered no sightseeing tours, and when I asked for a map, I was told: 'This is withdrawn for security reasons.' The sensible part of me said, 'The clock is ticking on my book, I've only got a month left in India, I haven't got time to waste on this dump,' but the stubborn 'I'm a travel writer and I better do my job' part decided that there must be *something* good about Jammu and I had a duty to stay and find it.

My first gambit was the old Fort, five kilometres above the town. This had lots of monkeys and a gauntlet of incredibly damaged beggars in an orderly queue leading up to the small Kali Temple within. 'You are so lucky!' my rickshaw man told me. 'Today Tuesday. Big *puja!'* But I didn't feel lucky. All I saw was a tiny, black-faced, flower-decked goddess figure and a small pen full of families earnestly praying to goats. 'Before, we kill goat for sacrifice,' explained a local priest. 'Now we rent out by the hour. Goat live to see another day!'

Fortunately, just below the fort, I found something I did like about Jammu. This was the lovely Bagh-I-Bagh gardens, a green and relaxing picnic spot constructed on a series of terraces and giving fine views of the Tawi bridge and the river. Calm and tranquil, it was the only place in Jammu where I felt completely safe and comfortable.

But I wasn't left long without the jitters. At my final stop, the Dogra Art Gallery, I found the small garden forecourt full of riot shields, helmets and batons, with the disrobed policemen having their lunch. The gallery itself was full of army clerks busily filling out supplies requisition forms for what looked like an impending crisis. 'Okay, that's it,' I thought. 'Time to get out of Jammu!'

*

Having haggled my rickshaw driver out of his 8 rupee 'government tax' – a very crucial saving as it turned out – I jumped on a 2pm bus south to Pathankot. And found that I had jumped from the frying pan into the fire. Pathankot was without doubt the noisiest, most unsafe place I had ever been to – even worse than Jammu. Grim, shifty-eyed figures began to circle me as I nervously backed into the nearby railway station. They seemed particularly interested in my bags. Fortuitously, after just two hours holed up in the railway station, a bus to *Manali* turned up. The cost of a ticket? Sixty-three rupees. How much money did I have left? Sixty-eight rupees. With all the banks closed, I could have been in big trouble had I not challenged the rickshaw driver for that 8 rupees earlier!

So relieved I was to have caught that bus that I launched into a spirited *gongyo* while waiting for it to leave. The driver and his rowdy mates heckled and made fun of me, then quietened down. In fact, as we set off on our long 12 hour night journey, they really looked after me – kept moving me into progressively better seats, until – at the end – I was in a window seat right behind the driver, with loads of leg room and fresh air and good views. This, they said, was the 'VIP seat'.

As the night progressed, I reflected that – by the time I reached Manali – I would have sat 27 hours in two days on hard-seated local buses. The downside of this was that my bum was really playing up. On the upside, after the first couple of hours, my mind just sort of 'switched off'. Time became meaningless and the journey passed incredibly quickly. All sorts of thoughts and memories occurred to me while I was in this weird kind of mental 'stasis'. I thought, for example, that I had been travelling round India over a month now *alone,* and that I had found it increasingly easy to push out to other people – most of whom 'happened' to be interested in Buddhism. Then I recalled the very vivid dream I'd had back on Gulam's boat that I had not had since my childhood. It wasn't the recurring dream I'd had (since about the age of six) of jumping off the Titanic and watching myself being chopped into tiny pieces by its giant propeller. It was the other, even more vivid, dream I'd had of being a gypsy girl in Victorian London. In this dream, which I now felt sure must be a former life-time, I became a Fagin-like teacher who taught her children to go round old people's houses and steal from them. 'Maybe that's why I felt so drawn to helping and looking after old people this time round,' I briefly considered. 'What a horrible person I must have been!' The authorities had agreed with me in this dream and the gypsy girl – now a diseased old crone – ended up in London's infamous Newgate Prison, where another old crone began teaching her about Buddhism. 'It just makes sense to me,' I concluded in my mind, 'that we live and learn, and then we die and have a rest, then we come back to live and learn again – until we have rounded off all our rough edges and are contributing value to the planet each and every moment as Buddhas.'

Chapter 13

Manali Stitch-Up

I was looking forward to Manali. Nearly every travcller I'd spoken to – especially the beach freaks in Goa – had been raving on about it. And they all said the same thing: the weed was plentiful and it grew ten feet tall. But it wasn't the weed I was looking forward to. It was the *other* thing travellers had raved on about, namely that Manali was one of the best places in India to chill out. This sounded good to me. After 35 days of bruising travel, and hardly any sleep in 72 hours, I urgently needed to chill out.

Imagine my disappointment, then, when I arrived in this nirvana of all Indian destinations and had just about the least chill experience imaginable. Fighting my way through a barrage of touts at the bus stand, I moved into a very clean room at the Pineview Hotel, 200 yards up the road – and immediately had to move out again. A bearded hippy next door was blasting out Bob Marley on his hi-fi. Migrating to the other side of the building, I next got a room outside which a team of workmen were demolishing an old house and putting up a new hotel. I eyed them dangerously, and they kindly downed tools and let me get some sleep.

I woke up three hours later to a pleasant surprise – it was warm and sunny. In fact, after the excesses of Calcutta (too hot) and Kashmir (too cold), the climate was just about perfect!

I had good connections in Manali. First, there was the exceptionally helpful tourist officer who deluged me with information and lent me fifty rupees until the banks re-opened after lunch. Then a couple of passing Canadians guidcd me up the back of the new town to Old Manali village. This was a lovely walk, particularly round the small iron bridge connecting the old and new towns. The landscape here was a pastoral delight of colourful meadows, brick-house water-wheels, rushing mountain streams, and snow-capped peaks.

Five minutes up the shepherds' path at the far side of the bridge, I came to the village of Old Manali. Here, life proceeded as it must have done for several centuries. Bales of hay hung out to dry from barnyard rafters, smoke drifted up from stove-chimneys poking from slate roofs, and stacked woodpiles propped up the sides of ornately-carved traditional village houses. Heading up to the top of the village via a damp cobbled path, I came to a ridge overlooking a winding river valley of beautiful flowers and meadows. It was a photographer's dream.

Appropriate then, that I met a young photographer from London called Robert who lived down in that valley. He was renting a 'house' with his girlfriend Pippa for just 20 dollars a month and he invited me to come visit them. Twenty minutes later, I was drinking tea and smoking my first *charas* with my new pals in their simple bare room (no furniture, just a single wood-stove) and learning all about Manali.

'There was nothing here 20 years ago,' said Robert. 'Just the old village. Then, in the '60s, the hippies found it—or rather its primo grass—but no other foreigners or tourists came here until the late 70's, when a ghastly new town sprang up to accommodate Indian honeymooners and noisy 'party people' wanting to be near the mountains.'

'And too scared to visit unstable Kashmir,' added Pippa, waving a billow of stove smoke away from her dark, sunburnt features. 'Bet you didn't see many Indians there, Frank.'

'No, I didn't,' I said with a wry smile. 'And if I'd bothered to check the weather forecast, you wouldn't have seen *me* there either!'

Robert's big, rough hands began cutting up a loaf of bread. 'I'm getting the munchies. How about you?'

'We were last here five years ago,' said Pippa, handing him

up some cheese. 'And most of the hippies were rude, arrogant Italians who wore tribal war paint on their faces and "exclusive" outlandish clothing. They were trying to look cool and different. I thought they looked ridiculous.'

Robert grunted through his efforts. 'Well, they're far less hippied now – the new legislation against dope saw to that. One of them was caught with a half-kilo of grass recently and given the choice of ten years in jail or a fine of 100,000 rupees. Bye bye, Italian hippies!'

It was in a happy mood that I returned to my hotel and prepared for bed. Manali was the first place in India I'd come to that I could wholeheartedly embrace. Okay, I would have preferred to be here in April, when the flowers and foliage were at their best (and before the hordes of Indians descended in May) but it was the nearest thing to paradise I had seen.

*

Paradise didn't last long, however. Two days later, having well and truly chilled out in Manali (including a heavenly hot sulphur spring bath up in the village of Vashisht), I rose early and made my way to the bus stand, intent on catching the one and only bus to Simla at 8am. 'What can possibly go wrong,' I thought complacently. 'It's a quiet Friday, so there's bound to be seats.'

But the seats weren't the problem. The problem was Steve.

My thin, wispy-bearded nemesis from Bombay came up behind me as I was negotiating a ticket with the bus driver.

'Oh, hey there, man,' he addressed me in his familiar, irritating Australian drawl. 'How's the travel writing going?'

I spun around in confusion. What was Steve doing here? I knew he'd been heading for Manali a month ago. Had he been here all this time?

'I've been staying with a family up in Old Manali,' he said as if anticipating my questions. 'Is this guy giving you trouble or something?'

'He says the fare is a hundred rupees,' I said, gesturing towards the driver. 'I've only got ninety rupees and one slightly ripped 500 rupee note which he won't change. Have you got ten rupees?

'Yeah,' said Steve. 'But you don't want to be paying no hundred rupees, man. 'You got the fare right there. The fare is only ninety rupees. It says so in my Lonely Planet guide. It also says "Don't get ripped off by bus drivers demanding a hundred rupees."'

I stared at Steve. 'Oh, okay, can I borrow that book for a minute? I left mine in Darjeeling.'

'Sure, man. You can keep it. I'm done with it, anyway.'

Feeling now outraged that some con artist bus driver was out to fleece me out of ten rupees he had no right to, I grabbed the proferred guide, thrust it up to him in his cab, and stabbed the relevant page. 'Fare is *ninety* rupees, not a hundred, it says so here. Why you try to cheat honest travellers?'

The driver gave a tired look, and picked absentmindedly at a spot on his pockmarked face. 'Fare is one hundred rupees. You give me one hundred rupees.'

'I don't believe this,' I turned round to inform Steve, but Steve was gone. And by the time I'd finished scanning the horizon for him and turned back again, the bus had gunned up and sped out of the terminal like a speeding bullet.

A small, laughing face was waving at me from out the back window.

It was Steve.

My mind went into freefall. What the hell had just

happened? And what was I going to do now? I was supposed to meet Anna in Delhi in three days. How would that now be possible?

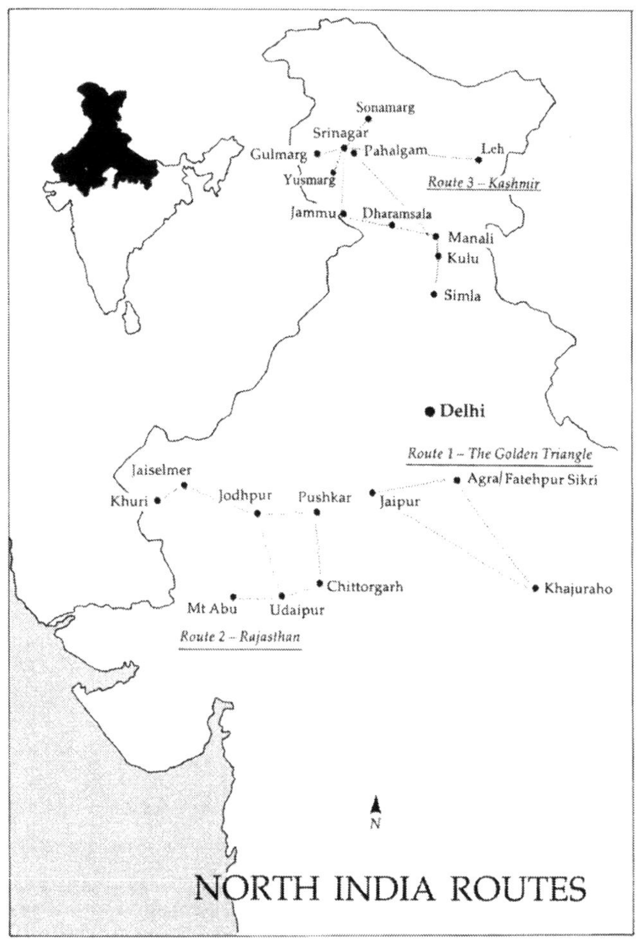

As I jumped impulsively on the next bus going south to Kulu – hoping against hope that I might catch up with my

Simla bus there – my brain was spinning. The more I thought about it, the more convinced I became that Steve had not been at that bus station by accident. Somehow, he'd known my movements and had set out to deliberately hijack me. Was I being paranoid? Yes, very possibly. But deep in my guts, I knew I was right. Steve had an agenda.

It went without saying that my Simla bus was not in Kulu – it had left long ago. There *was* a night bus out to Simla at 9pm, but that left me stranded in Kulu for 11 long hours. 'How am I going to fill my time?' I wondered as I sat in the small Monal cafe behind the tourist office. 'And why do I seem to be the only tourist in town?'

Also wondering where the tourists had got to were the general populace of Kulu – a thin-faced, grizzled collection of woolly-capped tailors, dentists, fruit and nut men, and shawl salesmen, all sitting or squatting patiently in their open shop-fronts. There would be no customers today.

The upside of all this was that unlike in touristy Manali, where I'd often got 'blanked' by locals, the people of Kulu were very open, friendly and keen to talk to me. In a little hut facing the pink-domed Shiva Temple on the riverbank separating old and new Kulu I found 'Baba', the resident priest. When I turned up, he was playing some eerie, mystical music with a few dope-happy pals on flute and drum. 'Come! Come!' he bellowed happily. 'You are from U.K. – correct?' I said that he was, and he said, 'I love the British. Princess Dianas! Rodney Stewarts! Michael Jaggers!'

Baba seemed a bit disappointed when I said I didn't know any of these luminaries. He was even more disappointed when I turned down a toke of his *charas*. But he was happy to mind my bag while I went off exploring, and directed me up the hill opposite to Kulu's principal landmark, the temple of

Raghunath.

Somehow, in the drizzling rain, I missed the temple and came instead to the Ambadi shawl factory. Looking in, I saw an industrious fellow on a handloom producing a very pretty woollen shawl. His name was Admika and he told me this shawl would take him 10 hours to produce – he had started at 7am, and expected to finish at 5pm. I hadn't been able to afford the expensive (up to Rs3000) pure *pashmina* shawls combed from the underbellies of Ladakhi goats I had seen in Manali, but this one – costing only 100 rupees – took my fancy, and over a cup of tea I ordered it for myself.

Then, to my surprise, one of Admika's pals, a schoolteacher called Om Prakash, invited me into his house to meet his family. While his kids played on my Walkman, I watched his wife repair garments on an old Singer sewing machine and noted little mice running in an out of the kitchen. I decided that I liked Kulu after all: the warmth and hospitality of this relaxed, happy family really made my day.

While I waited for the shawl to be completed, I found a second reason for liking Kulu. Heading further on up the hill – past the spooky old Transylvanian mansion known as Rapa Rupi Kullu – I came at last to a high ridge with stupendous views down over Kulu valley, the River Beas running down it like a silvery snake. A misty mountain range, enclosing the narrow valley on both sides, provided the perfect backdrop and I automatically reached for my small automatic Kodak camera. But then, as the winder refused to move on, I put it away again. 'Damn,' I pinched myself with regret. 'What a time to run out of film!'

Picking up my shawl on the way down, I returned to the Shiva temple just in time to join Baba and his chums as they performed their 7pm evening *puja* ceremony. Wood chips, incense and other offerings were cast into the blazing fire, and then Baba fished out a silver-topped conch shell and started blowing into it. 'We are purifying Shiva,' explained one of his acolytes. 'Then we are putting him to bed.' I looked at him askance. 'Blimey,' I thought as a mad ringing of bells and rattling of drums joined the loud hooting of the conch shell. 'I hope He's wearing earplugs.'

As I boarded the bus to Simla, I was still burning about Steve. I hoped I might find him there and not just pull out the hairs of his wispy beard one by one, but actually set fire to it and wipe that smug grin off his face forever. The last time I'd been tricked like this – losing all my pocket money on a 'Find the Lady' street card game when I was twelve – had scarred me so much that I had never bet on a game of chance since. This time, it was my faith in human nature that was at stake. Could I ever trust a 'friend' who offered help again?

I was also obsessing about Anna. In my mind I saw her emerging from Delhi airport – into the heaving, crazy throng of touts and rickshaw drivers outside the arrivals terminal – and getting right back on the plane home again. But then, as I silently chanted my fears away, I knew that she would be alright. Anna was made of sterner stuff. She'd faced down and calmed the maddest old codger – Old Bill – in the old people's home I'd run a few years earlier. India would not be a problem for her.

The moment my bus gunned out of Kulu's bus stand, however, I didn't have time to obsess about anything. Except survival. The bus driver was a single-minded maniac who stopped for absolutely nothing. And the whole road to Simla was winding, knife-edge bends along a mountain track hacked out of looming, overhanging rock. I was literally on the edge of my seat, hanging on for dear life, for eight long hours.

Chapter 14

Stressed out in Simla

Not surprisingly, we arrived in Simla early, at 5am. Too early to book a quick bus or train out again and too early, I was guessing, to even get some accommodation. But I needn't have worried. 'Porter!' announced a young man who came up to me on Simla's dark, silent Cart Lane. '*Government* porter!' I studied the anonymous brass token he thrust in my face and gave him a nod. 'Okay,' I said. 'Take me to hotel – cheap and best.'

His idea of 'cheap and best' was to lead me to three progressively grotty and expensive hotels – all of them up steep hills. 'Too much hill,' I grumbled at him. 'One more bad hotel and I look for myself.' My complaint was noted and porter boy promptly led me to the clean and affordable Hotel Ridgeview up on the Ridge, behind Christ Church. Here I was shown the best room I'd had in weeks (all the lights worked, it even had a waste paper bin) and I finally, after 24 hours, got some sleep.

I awoke five hours later, still fretting about Steve. Steve had seen my weakness. 'You're not very clued up, are you, man?' he'd chided me back in Bombay when I complained of not being able to sell my duty free fags, booze, and electronics on at a profit. 'This is Bombay, not Delhi. They already have all that stuff!' And just as I had not researched Bombay in advance, I had not researched *anywhere* in India in advance. All I did was collect mountains of tourist literature, stuff it in my bag without reading any of it, and move on to the next place. Steve must have known that the stupid Manali-Simla bus cost 10 rupees more than last season, and had shown me an out-of-date Lonely Planet guide.

'It's gone noon,' I grunted to myself. 'Time to hit Simla and go in search of that little git. He can't have gone far.'

But then I stepped out the hotel and my lack of research skills dealt me another blow. Simla was *massive* – finding Steve here would be like finding a needle in a haystack. Also, and this was an even bigger surprise, Simla was not a sleepy, semi-suburban, Victorian-type residential town at all, and not on the 'flat' as I had imagined. Instead, I found a second Darjeeling – the same hill-station built on a series of ridges, the same concentration of most government offices, banks and restaurants in just one street – the Mall – and the same arduous hikes up or down very long staircases to get anywhere. The only real difference I could see was the prevailing 'Britishness' of the place – not just the English red-roofed cottages, Georgian-style houses and palatial summer residences of the Raj, but the almost 'seaside' flavour of the Mall itself. Here, as I went in search of the tourist office, I encountered bracing air, civilised promenades, ice-cream counters, and bright souvenir shops. 'Good Lord,' I thought, mystified. 'I don't know what this reminds me of more – Brighton Pier or some sort of transplanted Swiss-English village!'

It was on the Mall that I ran into trouble. The one thing about Simla I did remember from my Lonely Planet guide – before I foolishly gave it to Megan in Darjeeling – was that it had a crap map. It was such a crap map that not even the tourist office was marked on it. Consequently, when I saw a half-decent map of this largest hill-station in the world (yes, I had just learnt that from a passing tourist) I had no hesitation in taking a picture of it. And was promptly arrested. 'Picture no allow! snarled the bearded security guard who came up behind me. 'Give me camera *now!'*

Little did I know, but the whole town was under curfew owing to current Punjab riots and killings. He probably thought I was an undercover agent or a spy.

'I like your hat,' I said, eyeing the handcuffs coming my way. 'Is there anywhere round here I can buy one?'

The cuffs stopped in mid-motion. 'Give me camera *now,'* the question was repeated. But behind the previously hostile glare I saw a slight twinkle of amusement.

The smile did it. 'I was taking picture of your beautiful Mall,' I beamed at him. 'It reminds me of my home and family in U.K. Do you have picture of your family?'

Sixteen grubby pictures of the guard's extended family later, I was released from his custody with a handshake. I made a mental note of that – a big smile will get you just about anywhere in India.

But not at Simla's tourist office. 'Hello,' I addressed the officer on duty, flashing him my most winning grin. 'My name is Frank Kusy and I am writing a travel guide on India. Can you help me?' The look of terror, combined with hostility, that crossed his thin, moustachioed features threw me completely. 'You are Frank Kusy? I no help you! You are bad man!'

This was not the reaction I had been expecting. 'I'm sorry,' I said, mystified. 'What have I done?'

'Mr Steve, he tell me! You take his money! You cheat him!'

I shook my head in bewilderment. This had all the makings of a very convoluted soap opera. 'Mr Steve – if this is the same Mr Steve we are talking about – is a liar. Look, here is my money belt. It is nearly empty. Mr Steve cheat *me.* What else he tell you?'

The frightened figure edged closer. 'He ask me lot of questions about Simla. Then he give me one card.'

The one card came slowly out of a drawer and I studied it. 'Steve Dobbs,' it said. 'Lonely Planet Travel Writer.'

To say my gob was smacked would be an understatement. Steve was working for Lonely Planet? So that was his game! He was trying to sabotage me and my book so that his own could prevail!

'This Mr Steve,' I asked quickly. 'When was he here?'

'He leave one hour before. He catch early bus to Delhi.'

'When is next bus to Delhi?'

'Today is limited service,' said the officer. 'No more bus till 9.30pm. You can take train.'

But the train was denied me. The Rail Reservation Office, just down the hill from the tourist office, was apologetic. 'So sorry, tourist quota for today is full. Can give ticket for tomorrow only.'

I sighed. This was turning into a highly frustrating version of *Around the World in Eighty Days,* with me as Passepartout and Steve as an elusive Phineas Fogg. And with him always just one step ahead.

I had a decision to make. Either I could hop on that late night bus to Delhi and try and track down Steve before he did any more damage. Or I could choose not to destroy myself with yet another marathon road trip and arrive in Delhi well rested for Anna.

I chose Anna.

*

Simla's railway station, where I turned up the next day, was a revelation. 'Good Lord,' I marvelled. 'This must be the only place in India where the best views of a town are from its railway station!' And it was true, the views of the valleys, as well as of Simla itself, were unparalleled. I also took delight in the quaint little railway sidings here with their charming narrow gauge engines and carriages. They reminded me of my childhood, when the days of the steam locomotive were still at their height.

The five hour trip down to Kalka on Simla's famous toy train was like travelling in a fairy tale – small size coaches, sofa-like seats, magnificent mountain views, and a long succession (102!) of hobbit-like tunnels. 'If there was anything the British did good in India,' remarked Graham, the only other Westerner on board, 'this railway track was it!'

On the connecting sleeper from Kalka to Delhi (left 11.40pm), I remembered all the night trains I had taken with Kevin last year and took up my familiar pose on the top bunk – earplugs in, eyeshades on, scarf over head (against fan draught), large bag tucked under legs, shoulder bag my 'pillow'. Then, because some Indians were having a party next door, I took a sleeping tablet and passed out for the next six hours.

I was still dozing when, at 6.30am, we drew into Old Delhi station.

Chapter 15

Anna

March 3rd had long been ringed in my diary. I was going to meet Anna in Delhi. I felt curiously unemotional about this reunion. That in itself was cause for concern.

After a horrid greasy omelette with Graham in the station restaurant, I snuck up on the roof of the YMCA in Jai Singh Road (my first ever accommodation in India) and did a good morning *gongyo*. Then, after changing my last $100 bill into rupees, I laid siege to the Poste Restante behind the main GPO in Bhai Vir Singh Marg. I wasn't going anywhere in Anna's direction until I was sure where she was staying. And until I was sure she would be awake.

The moment the Poste Restante opened its doors at 9am, I rushed in and laid claim to a clutch of letters – one from Paula (pleased with my Calcutta report), one from my mum (displeased with me for not writing more), one from Kevin (now chanting hard for a girlfriend), and three from Anna. Here I learnt – shock horror – that her March 2nd flight had been changed to March 1st. She had been in Delhi two days already! I also learnt that she would be staying at my old haunt, the Hotel Chanakya, which she said she had read about in my 'Kevin and I' book.

But if the letters from Anna unsettled me, they were as nothing to the postcard I read next. It was from Megan:

Dear Frank, I have been travelling with my friend Mary for the last four days in the Arun Valley. We are presently staying in a Sherpa village which won't make us food because we are white and 'caste-less'. Ha ha, problems, problems! Look, I'm writing to you because I bumped into Steve after you left Darjeeling. Yes, Steve from Bombay. And he is NOT what he seems. I found him talking into a tape recorder very much like your Walkman and when I asked him what he was doing he said he was working for LONELY PLANET. I'm sorry, Frank, but I'd already given him your whole itinerary from Darjeeling. He said he had lots of information for your book and was keen to hook up with you somewhere. Am thinking of you, and hope you work things out. Love, Megan xxx

'Ah ha,' I thought as the penny dropped. 'So that's how Steve knew to trip me up in Manali. And I bet he's got lots more trips in mind!'

Then I came to the end of the thin, heavily-postmarked card and received another shock.

P.S. it said. *I'm thinking of coming down to Rajasthan to meet you and Anna.*

The implications of this were mind-bending. Having just got the hang of travelling alone in India – in fact, enjoying my independence immensely – I was now faced with the prospect of two ladies descending on me at once! I felt very divided, and wrote immediately to Megan to explain my situation. I also suddenly realised that I would have to 'come clean' to Anna about Megan, and as soon as possible. It might blight her holiday, but I owed her the truth.

A short rickshaw ride down to Paharganj later, I tapped on the door of room 34 at the Chanakya. 'Who is it?' said a soft, familiar voice from within. 'It's me,' I replied. 'The man who is two days late in welcoming you to India.'

The door opened and Anna leapt into my arms with a shriek of joy. 'Oh, *there* you are, Frank!' she said happily. 'And I expected no less. You'd be late for your own funeral!'

It was a queer reunion. Anna's life went out wholeheartedly to me; my own was split down the middle. Half went out to her, half remained behind. Not so much the silent barrier of Megan, more the sudden, stubborn refusal to let go of my prized independence and freedom. From the start, I saw Anna as an obstacle to my continued enjoyment of India, rather than an aide and friend.

I began to explain why I had been late – about Steve and the missed bus to Simla, about not knowing about her changed flight until today – but Anna wasn't interested. 'Jump in the shower, sweetie,' she said with a sniff. 'You do smell a bit. Then let's go out and have lunch. I have such a lot to tell you!'

After my shower, during which Anna chattered away about sacred cows, I quickly sorted out my bags and sent ten kilos of excess baggage – 22 cassette tapes, 19 camera films and loads of tourist information – off to the U.K. via the excellent parcel packing service in Main Bazar. Then, feeling considerably 'lighter', I took Anna for a blow-out meal at the nearby Metropolis restaurant. This rooftop restaurant was as swanky as Main Bazar got and it had what had to be the longest menu in India—actually, four separate menus (Continental, Indian, Thai and Chinese) with a total of 146 dishes. All four menus were positively littered with quaint mis-spellings, notably BACKED MIXED PUMPKIN, POTATO POO MARY, CAPO CHINO (a pair of mafia trousers?), SWIEBING WITH KON (no idea) and, our favourite, MIXED FRUIT CRAPS WITH CHEESE RUMP SOUCE.

While we were waiting for our food, Anna asked me about my travels and how my book was going. 'It was going fine,' I replied. 'I was building up a guide to India which would have knocked Lonely Planet out of the ball park. But then I met a

character called Steve who *was* Lonely P
turned out to be writing for Lonely Planet. H
I was late meeting you in Delhi, and he's out th
right now trying to trash me and my reputation.'

Anna reached over to clasp both of my hands. 'W
you stop angsting about this guy and chant for his happ
she suggested. 'You know it's the right thing to do.' I d
know about that. The only thing likely to make Steve happ
would be for me to phone Paula, admit my defeat, and let Lonely Planet stomp a big hobnail boot on my book. But in my heart I knew Anna was right. Holding a grudge was like drinking poison and expecting the other person to die. Somehow, if I wanted to stop suffering, I had let go of my fear and resentment, and to respect Steve's life as I would a Buddha. A small, sneaky, highly irritating Buddha, but a Buddha nonetheless.

'Okay, I'll try,' I said as our food came into view. 'But how about you? How have you been coping here on your own?'

'Oh, I've been fine. Though trust me to arrive in Delhi on a Saturday. It was market day, and the streets were packed. I walked all the way up Main Bazar, taking care not to fall down big holes in the ground, and then I found a place that sold fresh fruit juice and just collapsed.'

I gave a brief nod of agreement. 'Yes, there's nowhere noisier than Main Bazar on a Saturday. It's just one big riot of noise, colour, dust and buzz.'

'It was the smells of the city that struck me first,' continued Anna. 'A mixture of rotten fruit, stale urine, sickly-sweet incense and dense diesel fumes from passing taxis. Then it was all the noises, a mind-numbing cacophony of blaring horns, shouting pedlars, ringing bicycle bells and barking, mooing, snorting animals. All you feel like doing, if you have any it all in. It takes some time, but fades into the background and place is so overwhelming that you hate it, you're best off you like it, you just say to road movie and I've just o happen *next*?" Then the l and begins to work for

happy that night, a big goofy grin plastered across her pretty, freckled features. But despite diversions like telling a street beggar about Buddhism, then making love twice, I knew I would have to tell her about Megan. At least if she knew, we could challenge the situation together.

*

I broke the news at midnight, and immediately regretted it.

'Erm, do you remember that dream you had about me and Megan?' I started quietly. 'You know, the one about me falling for her and having a relationship?'

Anna stirred in my arms. Then sat upright.

'Well, it came true,' I continued. 'Though "relationship" is hardly the right word. It was just the once, and it only happened because we were stuck up a 2000ft mountain in an icy lodge with nothing to keep us warm except each other. I'm so sorry, Anna, it won't happen again.'

The look of hurt and disappointment that crossed my loved one's face was heart-breaking.

'So, I was right,' she murmured softly. 'Those dreams of mine can be such a curse. The thing is – and please be honest here, Frank, as much to yourself as to me – do you still have feelings for Megan?'

I wished she hadn't asked me that. 'I…I don't know,' I stuttered miserably. 'I'm not in the habit of sleeping with people I don't fancy, so I guess I still feel an attraction. But one thing I *do* know is that I don't feel guilty. I'm very, very sorry I've caused you suffering, but I chanted about it and really felt the universe had put this person in my path for a good reason.'

Anna's sceptical look told me that I might be digging myself into a hole.

'What I mean is,' I added hurriedly. 'They say that if there isn't a crack in a relationship, there's no room for a third person to get in. Well, we've been skirting round the issue of marriage and kids for nearly three years now, and let's *both* be honest here, neither of us are ready. You've been married before and didn't like it. I'm embarking on a career as a travel writer and likely to be all over the world for the foreseeable future. What husband and wife material are we?'

'So what do we do now?' Anna's shoulders sagged in reluctant agreement. 'Put it all behind us and try and make the best of our time in India?'

'That would be nice,' I said. 'And let's bear in mind: there is no crack that cannot be repaired.'

We talked till 4am, slept fitfully until 9.30am, and woke up tired and emotionally exhausted. Then, following an uncomfortable *gongyo*, we had the most stressful and frustrating day imaginable.

It started with a city-wide strike of auto-rickshaws – a protest against recent Punjab killings – which left us struggling through hot, crowded Delhi on foot. Then, having finally reached the Air India building in Janpath I endured an appalling one and a half hour wait to book my return flight to the U.K. 'Go next door,' I instructed Anna at last. 'Tell Mr Chopra, the Assistant Director of Tourism, that I am unavoidably detained for our appointment.' Ten minutes later, Anna returned. 'Mr Chopra won't see you,' she said. 'Someone told him you are writing bad things about India.' I grimaced. 'Two guesses who that someone is.' I said with more than a snap in my voice. 'And you said to chant for his happiness.'

Things went better at the Delhi Tourism Development Corporation in Connaught Place. But only marginally. Steve hadn't got to this place yet, so the tourist officer agreed to see me. Only problem was, he kept *talking* about how he could help, but not actually doing it. Worst of all, there appeared to be no official guidebook on Delhi. 'Last printing is in 1982', he shrugged, reaching into a drawer and pulling out a large pile of papers. 'We have draft update sheets only.'

I felt bad about grabbing those draft update sheets from his hands and legging it out of the building. 'No, don't tell me off,' I apologised when Anna finally caught up with me. 'I'll transcribe what I need tonight and have them back in the morning.'

The 'Delhi by Night' city tour we took later on started well. We were the *only* people booked on it and got a private car. Even better, we got a personal trained guide all to ourselves. But then, after a pleasant stop at the colourful Laxmi Narayan Temple on Mandir Marg, we were dropped off at Delhi's famous Red Fort for its 7pm Sound and Light Show…and things turned bad again. 'This is eight rupee VIP seats,' said our guide importantly, showing us to the plush seats at the back of the spacious lawns. 'Much better than four rupee seats for poor people.' What he neglected to tell us, as the majestic buildings of the huge red sandstone fort were brilliantly illuminated one by one (with a booming voiceover) was that these premier 'garden seats' attracted all the mosquitoes. Or that they had a particular predilection for Western women who wore strong cologne and no insect repellent. 'Oh dear,' said Anna as we stood up at the end for a stirring anthem. 'I think they've got me.'

They certainly had. Twenty or so angry bites now covered her legs and ankles. And that was not all. Anna had just confessed to brushing her teeth with tap water that morning. Result? She became very ill. Back home at the Chanakya, she threw up all over the balcony. Then she was in the bathroom for two whole hours. 'Shall I try and find a doctor?' I said through the door. 'No,' she moaned miserably. 'Just pass me another roll of loo paper.'

*

Anna woke up the next morning completely drained by her illness. I did manage to coax her out to the nearby Lords Café for breakfast but one look at the menu – in particular, a novelty item called FRIED PORK GOBLETS – and she threw up again. 'You're staying in bed today,' I told her firmly. 'I'm off the chemist to get you some medication.'

Fortunately, I returned with not just some medication, but with a pharmacy doctor whom I had persuaded out of his practice for a few minutes. I say 'fortunately' because as soon as we got back to my room there was a loud clattering of footsteps behind us and three uniformed policemen crashed into the room also. 'Where is *drugs?*' demanded the grim-faced sergeant. 'Where is location of *drugs?*'

I rolled my eyes. Only one person could be responsible for this.

'There are no drugs,' I said wearily. 'Unless you count the penicillin this doctor has given me for my sick wife.'

'She is heroin addict!' accused the sergeant. 'Look! See! She is sweating and palpitating!'

'She has fever,' said the doctor calmly, holding his hand to Anna's forehead. 'Now, Deepak, *chale jao*, get out! Or I must tell your father you are taking bribes from informers again!'

All the wind went out of the policeman's sails. 'Oh, I am sorry Mr Singh,' he stuttered. 'I did not see this is you. Please, accept my apologies. I am going before I am coming.'

As the tricky trio exited the room, I spotted something peeping out of Deepak's back pocket.

It looked like the tip of Steve's familiar mauve-coloured business card.

Over a non-cow 'Lamburger' later, I was fretting at all the things and places I should be seeing in Delhi, but hadn't. 'I was here last year with Kevin,' I told Anna. 'But we didn't really take much in. Kevin was preoccupied with finding a cheese sandwich and I spent most of my time dodging crazy traffic and trying not to fall down holes in the road. This time it's different. I'm running against an almost impossible clock and really should be out there checking out the city.'

Anna nodded weakly. 'I understand. You've got a job to do. Let these pills kick in and then we'll do a little sightseeing.'

I wasn't sure about that, but let her join me anyway. After a whistle-stop tour of the better hotels (there weren't many) we visited the huge mosque known as the Jama Masjid in Old Delhi ("WOMEN ONLY ALLOWED WITH RESPONSIBLE MALE RELATIONS"), where we were grilled by three separate people to buy a one rupee camera ticket. Then an uninvited 'guide' tried to claim twenty rupees for following us up one of the minarets and back down again. If it wasn't for the superlative views over the old city from the top I would have made his descent a lot quicker with the end of my boot.

On Anna's suggestion, we revisited the Red Fort to take in its daytime action. She loved the bustling markets and in particular the beautiful Pearl Mosque behind the Royal Baths which had been constructed by the Emperor Aurangzeb for private worship in 1622. 'It's a real little gem!' she said in her first real display of enthusiasm. 'And so well preserved!' For myself, all that I hadn't seen before was a cow mowing the lawn, a performing monkey doing somersaults, and a goat balancing one-legged on a tree stump. The magicians in the 'entertainment area' at the back of the fort were truly talented.

Having popped the Delhi guide 'draft update' sheets back to the DTDC office in Connaught Place (they were *very* useful) I fell to fretting about Steve again. We would be heading off to Agra shortly – what other nasty surprises might that supercilious little pest have in store for me there? In my mind, I began considering alternatives. What if I changed my route and went to Jaipur instead to outwit him? But no, with Anna so sick, and with her worried that she might have to fly home to the U.K. before seeing the Taj Mahal, that was not an option.

Agra it would have to be.

Chapter 16

The Biggest Plastic Spider

One thing I remembered about Agra was all the aggravation. As a friend of mine, Joney, had remarked: 'There are two kind of mosquito in Agra. One is small mosquito. Other is big mosquito, like man. He say: "You want change money? You sell something? You want marble shop? Don't buy anything, just looking!'

'These touts really are like mozzies too,' I told Anna as we boarded the 7am Taj Express to Agra and ejected two lady squatters from our seats. 'Once they've got a fix on you, they won't let up until they've drawn blood. I was once stalked by a so-called "tourist guide" who insisted on coming into a gem factory with me. "You stay outside!" I told him and he said, "Why?" I looked him up and down and said, "Because I'm not paying your 40 per cent commission on purchases, that's why!" His response was classic: "No, no! We don't have commissions. We only have *incentives!*"'

Fortunately, we were able to circumvent all of this hassle by buying tickets on the train for one of the best conducted bus tours in India. It spun us round the three big attractions of Agra – Fatephur Sikri, Agra Fort, and the Taj Mahal – with hardly a tout in sight. Even better, since Anna was too ill to go hotel hunting, it made a good lunch stop at the wonderful old-style Clarks Shiraz hotel where the manager, Takosh Chakraborty, gave us a swish double room for just £10. 'Thank *God!*' said a relieved Anna, dumping her bag on the crisp-sheeted bed and dashing for the marble-tiled toilet. '*This* is the kind of hotel you should put in your book!'

Fatephur Sikri, we liked. Commenced in 1569 by Emperor Akbar as a grateful tribute to the celebrated saint Shaikh Salim Chishti (who successfully predicted the birth of three sons to his childless wives) and deserted just 14 years later (probably owing to water shortage) this finest of India's ghost towns – with its 500 beautiful palaces and buildings – was so untouched by time that it required only the slightest bit of imagination to visualise how it must have been 400 years ago, a refined and elegant court capital. 'How come it was never destroyed by later invaders like other Moghul cities?' I enquired of our guide. 'Oh, that is easy,' he said with a grin. 'It is 25 miles from Agra in middle of nowhere. They cannot find it!'

Next up was the massive red-turretted fortress of Agra Fort, built by Akbar between 1565 and 1573, and much added to by his son, the talented drunkard Jehangir. Here our guide took salacious delight in showing us one further addition – the lovely Sheesh Mahal (Mirror Palace) built by Jehangir's son, Shah Jahan. 'Look! See!' he said as he pointed us to the family-style Turkish bath with its myriad tiny lamps and tinkling rose-scented fountains. 'Akbar much like the ladies. Here he enjoy hot and cold dips with his wives. When local chieftains come to fort, he enjoy hot and cold dips with their wives and daughters also!' I enquired if this was the full extent of his sexual peccadilloes and the guide shook his head furiously. 'No! Next we see ladies' market of Meena Bazaar. Here Akbar dress up in feminine disguise so he can mix up with feminine sex!'

Before leaving the fort, we were shown the tiny, gold-domed turreted room where Shah Jahan – deposed by his son

Aurangzeb – spent the last 12 years of his life, looking over the River Yamuna to the still, shimmering mirage of the Taj Mahal. 'Oh, what a perfect preview,' said Anna, clapping her hands together with glee. 'I can't wait to see the real thing!'

She didn't have to wait long. Half an hour later, our bus drew up outside the most famous monument to love the world has ever seen. The crowning achievement of Shah Jahan, it was built to immortalise the memory of his beloved wife Mumtaz, who died tragically in 1631 giving birth to her 14th child.

'Don't bolt down to see it at close quarters,' I said with a smile. 'Check out the mammoth entrance gate first. Shah

Jahan's tragic prayer "Help us, O Lord, to bear that which we cannot bear" is inscribed on it.'

But Anna was already on the move. 'Oh, but it's beautiful!' she called back as she passed the sweeping green lawns and fountains, and came to the huge domed mausoleum with its two side mosques and four minarets. 'It looks like it's floating against a backdrop of empty sky!'

I nodded as I caught her up. 'That was a conscious device, I think, to produce the illusion of a palace seemingly suspended in the air. And you don't have to be romantic to fall in love with the Taj – it moves even hardened cynics like me.'

As we passed inside the cool cenotaph chamber where the 'dummy' tombs of Shah Jahan and Mumtaz were located (the real ones, to avoid looting, were placed in the dark, humid basement chamber below), Anna found herself compulsively stroking the walls. 'The marble has such a supple, sensual quality,' she commented. 'I keep wanting to touch and caress it!' Something else she could not help doing, as we took photographs outside and prepared to leave, was look over her shoulder. 'I have to keep assuring myself it's real,' she said in a low murmur. 'It's one of those few times in life when fantasy and reality perfectly coincide.'

After a quick POPEYE WITH TOM ONION (papaya with tomato and onion) at Joney's Place behind the Taj I had to bring Anna back down to Earth again. 'It's time to hit the tourist office,' I told her. 'And if Steve's been there already – which I very much expect – it's not going to be pleasant. You can go back to the hotel if you want.'

But Anna wasn't going anywhere. Loyal as ever, she tagged along. And when we got to the Government of India tourist office on the Mall, there was no armed guard in evidence. Nor even the offer of a close arrest. Instead, I was greeted by a small, sleepy tourist officer who hadn't heard of me at all. 'This is strange,' I whispered to Anna as he began ferreting around for a map of the city. 'Steve must know I'm in Agra today. Why hasn't he sabotaged me again?'

As if on cue, a scruffy urchin with a toothy grin tugged at my sleeve. 'Your name is Mister Frank?'

I jumped back at this strange intervention. Then looked down and took the slip of paper that was being thrust at me.

Hey Frank, it said. *I'm in hospital. Need your help bad. If you get this, follow this boy. Steve.*

p.s. Sorry for all the shit, man. Will explain.

'You are going to help him?' said Anna, leaning over my shoulder to read the note. 'He sounds like he's in real trouble.'

I bristled. 'Well, he's *caused* real trouble. If not for him, I could have been in Delhi a day earlier and stopped you drinking that dodgy shower water. Not to mention all the trouble he caused yesterday with those even dodgier policemen.'

But as the boy tugged urgently at my sleeve again, I knew what I must do. 'Okay,' I sighed. 'Lead me to Mister Steve…'

*

The young reception nurse at the Shanti Mangalick Hospital in Fatehabad Rd was surprisingly welcoming. 'Ah,' she said as I introduced myself. 'So you are Mister Steve's friend! He will be so happy to see you!'

Friend? I didn't know about that. It was going to take all my restraint not to wring his scrawny neck the moment I set eyes on him.

'What's his problem?' I asked casually as we moved up the spic and span wards. It looked like the hospital had just been built.

'His problem is rabies,' said the nurse just as casually. 'He have it for some time.'

Anna and I stopped dead in our tracks. 'Rabies?' we said in unison.

'Yes, some dog bite him four, maybe five, weeks ago. He should have vaccine treatment immediately. Too late now.'

'Too late?' we echoed again. 'What do you mean, "too late"?'

'Almost one hundred per cent, human rabies is fatal,' said the nurse, looking suddenly serious. 'Mister Steve, he must die.'

*

The small, wan figure in the dark, quiet room was instantly recognisable.

'Hi guys,' slurred Steve, slowly propping himself up on a

pillow. 'They got me on diazepam to control my err…muscular spasms and excitability. Talking of moving me onto morphine if I get any worse. Then I'm a gonner going nowhere.'

'So you know your condition?' I said slowly.

'Oh yeah, I know. Damn dog. Came at me out of nowhere. Caught me stroking one of its pups. And it weren't a bad bite, just a nip. Guess I should have taken it more seriously…'

'You think?' I said with more than a note of incredulity in my voice. 'You're a travel writer, for God's sake. You've been round this country a dozen times and you ignore a dog bite?'

'I knew there was something wrong,' said Steve, brushing aside the admonition, 'when I began stitching you up at those tourist offices. And especially that shit I laid down with the Delhi policemen. I told them to just scare you, maybe lock you up for a night, but that wasn't me. That was the bug kicking in. I've been saying, doing, all kinds of irrational shit. Paranoid hallucinations, they've been doing my head in. I thought you were another Lonely Planet writer out for my job. You got to get me out of here, man. I don't want to die in this place!'

'He no go anywhere,' the nurse whispered to us. 'He is having convulsions in the street when they bring him in.'

All my rage at Steve melted into pity. Karma had caught up with him and there seemed to be no way out.

'If I had my way,' I told him after doing a little chant in my head. 'I would pack you off to Delhi on the Taj Express tonight, and book you on a plane straight back to Oz. But the nurse here says you can't be moved. What say I ring your folks?'

Steve's face brightened. 'Oh, would you? That would be great of you, man. Here, let me write down the number…'

The phone call I made to Steve's parents in Sydney was the

toughest of my life. His mother cried, his father got angry and (I could hear in the background) started throwing furniture around. Then they both calmed down and said they would be on the first flight over to India.

'You've got a rich dad,' I told Steve on my return. 'He's not only coming with your mum tomorrow, he's bringing a top flight medic with a new experimental vaccine. Don't give up, mate. There's always hope!'

Tears of relief and gratitude sprang to Steve's eyes. 'Can't thank you enough, man,' he said, leaning painfully forward to shake my hand. 'Now let me do something for you.'

And with that he slowly opened up his rucksack and revealed its contents. 'Here you go. All my tapes and notes on Northern India. You can have them – they're no good to me now. I'll get my dad to phone Lonely Planet, explain the situation. They'll have another guy out soon, but it'll give you and your travel book the edge that you need.'

My eyes widened at such unexpected largesse. 'Are you sure?'

'Dead sure,' said Steve, regaining his composure. 'Now get out of here. I'll be fine from hereon in.'

Anna squeezed my hand as we departed the hospital. It was a meaningful squeeze which demanded a response. 'Yes, I know.' I said between gritted teeth. 'You said to chant for Steve's happiness, and you were right. But if things have worked out for me, they certainly haven't for him. He said to me once that India is like a lucky dip bag, that sometimes you don't get the sweetie, you get the plastic spider. Well, he's got the biggest plastic spider ever. I just hope he'll be okay…'"

Chapter 17

Everyone has the right to be a Hamster

The Superfast Express train we took to Jaipur turned out to be super slow. It was supposed to leave at 5.40pm, but only actually left at 7pm. Very puzzling. It did move once during this long delay. It went ten yards…backwards. Then, having shared some of the journey with a straggle-bearded, rolling-eyed *sadhu* (holy beggar) who kept offering us 'boomshanka', we encountered further delays and only crawled into Jaipur at 1am.

It was a good thing that I had access to Steve's notes. 'If on a budget,' he had written, 'you'll have to fight hard to get to a decent lodge. Rickshaw wallahs are highly inventive when it comes to placing you in dives which pay them commission. "My hotel," they'll say, "is very close (i.e. stuffy), with clean rooms (once a month), live entertainment (cockroaches), comfortable beds (for the bugs), fan in room (no power), bathroom (bucket) and western toilet (faces west)." This is your cue to feign deafness or to pretend intimate relationship with the city police chief. It's a great game, best played tongue-in-cheek, which you only win if you get to the hotel of your choice without throttling the rickshaw man. Upon reaching a good place like the Arya Niwas Hotel in Sansar Chandra Rd, he will feign astonishment, unable to believe that it has not (as previously stated) burnt down, closed down or been struck by cholera. He will apologise profusely and then he will suggest a good gem factory nearby.'

I chuckled to myself as we checked into our clean, comfortable room at the Arya Niwas. Under different circumstances, Steve and I could have really got on.

The 'Pink City' of Jaipur lies 250 kilometres west of Delhi and is famous for its Amber Fort, its many Mughal monuments, and in particular for its shopping. I had seen and done none of these things when I was here last year with Megan. My only pleasant memory of Jaipur had been of its ice cream.

Leaving Anna back at the hotel (she had been vomiting all night again, poor thing) I mentioned this to my rickshaw driver and he took me to the Kwality restaurant on M.I. Road. 'Number one place for ice cream!' he said, and he was right. I had three different flavour scoops in a row – checking out the fabulous décor (much like a Maharajah's *mahal*) as I did so – and then I noticed the restaurant's 'All you can eat for Rs28' lunchtime buffet. 'Ooh, this is nice,' I thought as I tucked into all ten dishes on offer. 'Those spicy Szechwan specialities look particularly good!' Minutes later, I changed my mind. 'Oh dear, my guts are rolling. I need to lie down!'

Back at the hotel, I found Anna all hot and sweaty and in a combative mood. 'The air-cooling box and ceiling fan packed in an hour ago,' she complained. 'Can't we find somewhere to stay that isn't subject to power cuts?' I explained that power cuts were part and parcel of India, especially in the dry pre-monsoon months, but she wasn't interested. 'What happened to all those 5 star hotels that were going to give you free stays?' she said accusingly. 'Why can't we stay in one of them?' I opened my mouth again, to say that these hotels depressed me – they weren't part of the 'real' India – but she was even less interested. 'Personally, I blame your *gongyo.*' she grumbled. 'You know, the bit you always stumble over?' I looked at her glumly. Whenever she put her Buddhist mentor cap on, I knew I was in for a lecture. 'See here,' she said, snatching up my daily liturgy book and stabbing at the relevant page. "Nyuwa shichi-jiki sha". That loosely translates as "Everyone has the right to be happy." Now I don't know exactly, my Japanese is a bit rusty, but I think what *you* are saying is: 'Everyone has the right to be a hamster."

I giggled at that. She had to be having a laugh. But no, this was Anna. She was quite serious.

'Your point being?' I said.

'My point being, that this makes perfect sense. You've been chanting for the privilege of being a hamster, and apart from that lovely hotel we had yesterday in Agra, you've been sticking us in small, hot, poky rooms that only a hamster would be happy in. All we need is a wheel!'

It was no good arguing when Anna was on a roll like this. To distract her, and to give her three hours of cool, uninterrupted air-conditioning, I took her to the Raj Mandir off M I Road. This premier movie-house of Jaipur, with its glittering deco lobby and flashing lights around the screen whenever the film reached a crescendo, was packed out with local families seeking their weekly escape from the noise and hype of the streets outside. Though the film on offer – *Main Tulsi Tere Aagan Ki* – which translated as 'I am the holy basil of your garden' – was totally inscrutable.

'What did you make of that?' I asked Anna as the blaring soundtrack finally fell silent.

'I'm not sure,' she said with a smile on her face. 'All I gleaned was that the hero's half-brother's mother was supposed to be a prostitute, but as it turned out she wasn't.'

On the street, walking back to the hotel, I noticed two new road-signs—one saying DEVELOP AQUARIUM FISH

HOBBY, and the second, TRY COBRA TRAINING COURSE. Then, further down, we came across a sweetshop selling an intriguing confection called MASTICABLES. 'What is *that*?' I asked the shop-keeper, and he said, 'twenty-five rupees, please!' Masticables, we learnt from the wrapper, came in four 'fun' flavours and their primary ingredient was bovine gelatine. What bovine gelatine did, as I discovered after trying the product, was weld my upper and lower jaws together after just one bite. 'The big plus to this, of course.' I remarked to Anna after I had finally prised my teeth free again, 'is that one pack of Masticables will you last a lifetime.'

It didn't take long for my blow-out buffet in Agra to catch up with me. I woke at 7am with diarrhoea. 'That'll teach you,' said Anna as we battled for possession of the toilet. 'You reeked of garlic when you came home yesterday. How much of that Chinese food did you pack away?'

I boarded the morning tour bus of Jaipur with some misgivings. The last time I'd had a gut attack on a bus – last year, travelling from Delhi to Kathmandu – had been a horror show. But I needn't have worried. A quick, intense chant for instant good health – coupled with a hefty dose of Codeine Phosphate – got me through the rest of the day with no further attacks.

The tour itself was excellent and completely revised my (previously poor) view of Jaipur. It started off at the high 18th century merchant's house called Nawab Sahib Ki Haveli, which afforded remarkable panoramic views of the whole city from its rooftop terraces. 'Maharaja Jai Singh II, he build Jaipur as "planned city"', said our guide, pointing us to all the broad, symmetrical main streets, neatly intersected by little narrow side roads. 'Then, in 1727, because old capital of Rajasthan, Amber, is too easy for Delhi people to attack, he make big wall all around city and make Jaipur his new capital.'

Anna and I marvelled at the distinctive pink-orange colouring of the city. Looking down onto the bicycle-infested Tripolia Bazaar every monument and building glowed a soft, romantic pink. 'Is that why Jaipur is called the "Pink City?" asked Anna. 'No,' grinned the guide, twirling the ends of his typically curled Rajasthani moustachios. 'In 1876, Maharaja Ram Singh he paint whole city pink to welcome your Prince of Wales and Queen Victoria as guests. Pink is colour of hospitality!'

After a short stop at the high pyramidical façade of Hawa Mahal – nicknamed the 'Palace of the Winds' because of the cool westerly winds which blew through its five storeys of overhanging windows – the tour moved 11 kilometres north to the Amber Palace. Here, as we surveyed this fairy-tale masterpiece of yellow sandstone set atop a craggy hilltop, Anna spotted the elephants. 'Oh, look, elephants!' she cried. 'Can we go up by elephant? It's only a hundred rupees!'

Only a hundred rupees? What a rip off, I thought. A hundred rupees was the cost of a room for the night, and although Anna had brought $300 dollars over to bolster my finances, that was going to have to stretch a long, long way. The look on her face, however, was impossible to deny. If she wanted an elephant, she was going to have one.

'Oh, this is wonderful!' she enthused as we swung up to the Fort on a howdah'd pachyderm. '*This* is more like the real India. Look, it's letting me stroke its trunk – it's just like leather!'

The main attraction at the top was the showpiece Shish Mahal or Mirror Palace, built by the astronomer prince Jai Singh II. The exterior was a studded jewel-box of polished mirror fragments, set in plaster. Within, glass mosaic panels and highly ornamented plaster reliefs, inlaid with glass and marble carvings, vied for attention. Further on, we came next to the magical Chamber of Mirrors (the world's finest) which used to be the Maharajah's bedroom. If anything, this was even more impressive – the whole ceiling was a glitter of tiny mirrors which, when illuminated by the guide's candle, produced a spectacular illusion of stars traversing a night-black sky.

Back in Old Jaipur, the tour called in at Jai Singh's most interesting legacy, the Jantar Mantar observatory. 'As an astrologer myself, I've been reading up on this,' I told Anna a little pompously. 'And the starstruck young ruler sent out scholars to foreign observatories in Britain, Greece, Arabia, and Portugal before realising his dream of India's greatest astronomical observatory here in Jaipur in 1728. Each of this strange collection of surreal, yellow-sandstone sculptures has a specific astronomical function, be it to measure the sun's declination, azimuth or altitude, or to determine eclipses or the declination of fixed stars and planets. Check out the 30 metre high sundial – it casts a shadow which moves some four metres each hour, giving the time down to two-second accuracy.'

Anna listened to this long discourse very patiently. Then she said: 'That's all very well. But what did they do when the sun wasn't shining?'

Our final stop – the Central Museum in the new city – was a real curiosity piece, full of bits out of medical colleges, birds that had fallen off their perches, and bald, stuffed animals. 'Is this the strangest museum you've come across in India?' smirked Anna through her exhaustion. 'Not quite,' I replied. 'That honour goes to the bizarre 'Science' museum I found in Udaipur last year. Visitors were welcomed in by a skeleton in a sari (with a fag in its hand) and the whole place was stacked with dusty exhibits, obviously stuffed by an amateur taxidermist. All those poor departed animals – their eyes were stuck on their heads more or less at random. Eyes that were totally the wrong size and the wrong shape. And the bodies had strange lumps and tears in the skins, as if they had been subjected to horrible scientific experiments. A lot of them had fallen off their stands and were just lying there with their feet in the air at the bottom of their cages, covered in dust and in the most unnatural poses. Like the mongoose with the pin up its bum, apparently bowing to Mecca. Or the giant stingray which they'd managed to cram into a milk bottle.'

I thought I'd heard all the cons and scams possible in India, but I was wrong. As we left the museum, we were accosted by a bogus English student who innocently enquired: 'Have you seen the elephants coming home from Amber?' I said 'No', and he told me of an area in the old city (below Surajpol Bazaar) where Amber Fort's 40 or so elephants bedded down each night. Interested, I asked where I could find it. This was the grinning tout's cue to produce, triumphantly, his jewel emporium card. The huge advantage of the Arya Niwas hotel, we decided on our return, was that it was right in the heart of Jaipur—one really felt the buzz of the city here, and the noisy rickshaw-wallahs, carpet sellers and tourist touts were at a safe distance, just around the corner. Run by a friendly, ultra-efficient Brahmin family—the Bhansals—it was a safe and peaceful oasis of calm, with a wide green lawn to relax in and the best budget food in town. It was also, I noticed, full of Western tourists. Every night, there was a small huddle of them to be found on the veranda, each clutching a brown paper bag full of duty-free booze (which the Bhansals frowned upon) and furtively swigging from it as they swapped travel tips and stories.

I joined this coterie tonight and got talking to an English guy called Terry, who was in Rajasthan to buy marble masonry. I asked Terry what he liked most about India, and he said 'Oh, that's easy – the total unpredictability of it! I mean, you just don't know what's going to happen next, do you? They say that everything is "no problem", but the problems are monumental. Which is why so many western buyers go under and the few that stick it out do so well. All these festivals and holidays they keep having is one major block to getting anything done, but *they* don't get uptight over it, so why should we? Everything is "tomorrow coming" or "nearly finish", so there's no point getting urgent over anything. You just have to take whatever timescale they give you, double it, and add three days!'

I made a mental note of that. This buying and selling thing in India sounded fun. Some day I might give it a try…

Chapter 18

Dollops and Darshan in Pushkar

At this point, I had a difficult decision to make. With Steve's treasure trove of information under my belt and with Anna still being so sick, I felt tempted to cut my trip short and haul us both back to the U.K. post haste. But Steve's notes mysteriously tapered out at Jaipur and I couldn't access his tapes since they were mini discs which wouldn't play on my Walkman. 'I really should have asked him if he'd covered Gujarat and the rest of Rajasthan,' I mentally castigated myself. 'Oh well, too late now. I'll have to see them for myself.'

One thing was for certain. I would have to see at least some of them *by* myself. Anna had bravely kept up with me, and my busy schedule, thus far. But each day saw her closer to total collapse. She had to rest up and recover somewhere, but where could that be?

'Oh, that's obvious,' said Terry, joining us for breakfast. 'Take her to Pushkar. You're going there anyway, right? And I'm heading most of the way there myself in a bit – why not hitch a lift with me in my Ambassador taxi?'

The relief on Anna's face was palpable. One more slow, sticky, crowded train journey and I felt sure she would scream.

We set out at noon, Anna sleeping on the back seat of the car while I squeezed up front with Terry and the driver. 'Get ready for the ride of your life,' grinned Terry, running a thin, bony hand through his short-cropped hair. 'Highway number 8 is the most dangerous road in India. It stretches in a more or less straight line all the way from Delhi to Bombay and attracts so many speed-crazed trucks—and consequently so many accidents—that Dudu, where we'll stop briefly for lunch, now has a weird little hut by the side of the road which dishes out prosthetic limbs – mainly legs, arms and elbows – to casualties of bus crashes. This hut is funded by a charitable organisation called "The Jaipur Limb Campaign", and it has been set up to provide for poor village people who cannot crawl from their accident site to the nearest hospital. No wonder then that the most popular seat on any bus going down Highway no 8 is the seat right behind the driver. Most Indians would rather die outright (along with the driver) than be mutilated.'

'Oh, *that's* why it's called the "VIP" seat', I interjected. 'I wondered why so many Indians have been honouring me with it!'

Highway no 8 was littered with dead pigs, dogs, birds and overturned trucks. It was also dotted with signs like ACCIDENT PRONE AREA and OVERTAKING MEANS UNDERTAKING, but nobody paid a blind bit of notice. Our maniacal driver was no exception. Hurtling down the highway like a man possessed, he only obeyed the 'Wait for Side' instruction on the lorries ahead when their drivers vigorously flapped their hands out of the window, indicating that drawing alongside was an invitation to certain death. And his attitude seemed to be: 'If we make it to our destination, God is with us, and if not, He must have been looking the other way.'

At the midway stop of Dudu I tried to score a cheese sandwich, and failed. 'Dudu is a really weird place,' warned Terry with a chuckle. 'Here you'll be lucky to find a waiter, let alone any food!'

Inside, the place reminded me of a railway waiting room

after the last train had gone – all empty and deserted, full of lonely echoes and with no furnishings at all. If it wasn't for the blue fridge lurking in one corner and the rack of dusty bottled drinks sitting in the other, I wouldn't have known it was a restaurant at all. I went outside and came back in again, hoping to attract some attention. This time, there was a low, muffled creaking sound at the back of the building, suggestive of some ancient, long unused door being slowly prised open. Then a swarthy, black-bearded waiter issued forth and began trying to sell me jewellery made by his sister one kilometre down the road. My request for a cheese sandwich fell on deaf ears.

'This is as far I go', apologised Terry at our next stop, Kishangarh. 'I have a lot of marble business to do here, along with buying the whole side wall of a mosque for a client in Dubai. But you can get a bus here to take you onto Pushkar. It's just down the road.'

Pushkar wasn't exactly down the road – it was half an hour on to Ajmer, and then a slow crawl by local 'pilgrim' bus over the 'Snake Mountain' of Nag Pahar – but I thanked him anyway. Yet again, a *shoten zenjin* (protective angel) had appeared to light my way.

On the bus, I began making revisions into my tape-recorder. On the surface, I reminded myself, Pushkar was just a peaceful little pilgrim town – population around 5000 – with a definite emphasis on rest and relaxation. Few visitors came for sightseeing and the little 'action' there was took place on the single long market street which tracked round the northern end of the 'holy' lake, parallel to the bathing *ghats*. Elsewhere, above this touristy main drag, was an extensive maze of mediaeval alleys, quaint old houses, sleepy backstreet temples (some guarded by aggressive monkeys) and shady banyan trees parked with dozy dogs, camels and cows. There were also impressive white-washed palaces and larger temples, mostly dating back to the 17th century, which had been tacked on by the Rajput Maharajas. Man Mahal, the palace built by Rajah Man Singh I of Amber as a hunting lodge, still stood on the bank of the lake and had been converted into the present Sarovar Tourist Bungalow. The original 100 or so temples, decorated by shapely cupolas, arches and pillars, opened onto bleached-white bathing *ghats* and ringed the lake. The backdrop of stark desert and two towering hilltop temples reinforced the feeling of being in a quasi-Mediterranean resort. For Brahmins, this was the holiest place in the world, and *every* devout Hindu attempted a pilgrimage here—to bathe and make an offering to the lake—at least once in a lifetime.

Okay, these were the facts – this was as far as most guidebooks went. Nothing, however, prepared the average visitor for the sheer eccentricity of the place. I remembered, for example, taking a room at the Tourist Bungalow when here last year. It wasn't a 'room' at all—just an octagonal castle turret with barely enough space to cram a mattress into. I opened the door and quite literally fell into bed. But hey, I wasn't complaining. Where else in the world could I score a palatial turret-room, with balcony views of the lake and glorious sunsets, for less than one English pound?

Nothing prepared one for the eccentricity of the people either – especially the shop-keepers. If the barrage of friendly one-liners didn't get you – 'Hello, fruit porridge! You are coming from? Change dollar?' – the plethora of music stores, second-hand bookshops, juice bars, German bakeries and relaxing restaurants surely would. From dawn to dusk, a regular parade of hippies and tourists trooped up and down the market—trying on clothing, buying silver bangles, drinking endless lassis, doing *puja* at the ghats, or simply collecting strange signs like: DONATE FOR COW SAINT (a temple), WELCOME TO SEE THE REAL MAC COY (a handicraft shop) and SURPRISING HOW A SINGLE NAME CAN CHANGE YOUR OUTLOOK (a cigarette advertisement). And everyone congregated at sunset, when the dry heat was relieved by a cool breeze and the fading desert lights turned the lake a fiery blood-crimson. As the time approached for *darshan* (putting the gods to bed) hundreds of tiny temples by the lakeside came to life and the air was filled with the clanging of bells, the beating of drums and the hypnotic drone of prayer. For many, this was the nearest they would get to a 'mystical' experience of India.

Terry was right about Pushkar. A charming oasis on the edge of the desert, it was the ideal place for Anna to rest up and recuperate. She was particularly enamoured of the Tourist Bungalow with its peaceful ambience, its peacocks on the lawn, and its faded rundown charm. 'Some of the rooms are huge and antique, with high domed ceilings and views of the lake!' she enthused as we took a quick tour. 'I'm spoiled for choice!'

She wasn't spoiled for long. At 6am – yes, 6am! – we were woken by a boisterous Indian family clattering about in a room two doors along. Kalimar, our German neighbour, and I both poked our heads out at the same time to investigate. 'Why do they get up so *early?*' said Kalimar. 'There is nothing for them to *do*!'

After an altercation with the Tourist Bungalow manager – who refused to move the Indian family to the other end of the building – I made the decision to move up the road to the refurbished Pushkar Hotel. 'You'll be happy here,' I informed Anna. 'They've added a smart new indoor restaurant, the bathrooms are tiled, and you can bask all day on the roof or on the green lawns. Oh, and if by some miracle you feel better, you can take a nice, gentle swim over to that little shrine in the centre of the lake from here. I did it last year.'

There was a sharp intake of breath from behind me. 'You swim in lake last year?' exclaimed the hotel manager.

'Yes, what of it?' I replied.

'But ees *crocodile* in lake!' he said. 'Nobody tell you of *crocodile?*'

My mind scrolled back to the event. 'I did hear people shouting "Crocodile! Crocodile!" at me from land, but I think they are joking.'

'You lucky man!' said the manager. 'Crocodile eat visiting official last year! They shoot it and put it in jail!'

'In jail?'

'Yus. I quick show you!'

And with that, he pulled me down to a small bathing ghat, just off the main market street, where Pushkar's last (late) crocodile resided—behind cast-iron bars—in a long open sarcophagus overlooking the lake. As he had indicated, I had been *very* lucky.

While I was out and about I decided to visit 'S.N.', the amazing barber opposite the Krishna restaurant. I was in his capable hands for over an hour – first a great haircut and shave, then a vigorous half-hour head massage. In fact, with all the lotion, powder, massage and cream, he made my head feel like a precious urn being turned on a potter's wheel.

Out of the barber's, a local shopkeeper sidled up to me and began fondling my close-shaven head. 'You look like a filmic actors!' he crooned.

'Really?' I said, shrinking back in alarm. 'Which one?'

'Tinu Anand! He is comedy like Mafia. Different, different roles. Now I call you Yograj Builder!'

'Yogras who?'

'This is bestest film of Tinu—"Kranti Veer"—and mostest famous role!'

I surveyed the small, manic figure before me. His eyes were bloodshot and rolling around with suppressed hysteria.

'What is your name?' I asked. 'And have you been on the local *bhang?'*

'My name Lalit Jain,' he giggled foolishly. 'And *bhang* is good. It bring me close to God!'

I didn't know about that. The last person I'd spoken to who'd had one of Pushkar's famous *bhang* lassis had complained of hallucinating so hard that his room was full of animals and a big waterfall appeared at the top of his shower. 'I was drowning in tiny, wet animals!' had been his sad comment.

'Come in my shop!' wheedled Lalit, his luminous pink shirt clashing wildly with his army camouflage shorts. 'It is cold, like super-computer! We can talk bullshit for the laughing, and you can digest your food like buffalo dinner!'

I promptly renamed him Mr Bullshit.

Back at the hotel, I found Anna still weak and looking very tragic. 'Where's your beard gone?' she complained. 'And why did you leave me alone for so long?' I said I was sorry – that Pushkar was full of distractions – then I tried to feed her some banana curd from the hotel kitchen. It stayed in her stomach precisely ten seconds before vomiting forth again. 'This is getting serious,' I said, concerned. 'Why won't you let me get you a doctor?'

Anna shook her head feebly. 'Let's do *gongyo,'* she said with a stubborn pout. 'I'm going to summon up the courage and wisdom to beat this thing myself.'

The only thing she summoned up, however, was her anger. 'You've got time for everyone else in this country,' she rounded on me afterwards. 'But not for me! Why can't you share anything with me?'

I felt like reminding her that she was stuck in a 10 x 12 ft room with an attached toilet, that it was difficult to share anything else with her while she was so sick. Instead, I sat gingerly on the edge of the bed and allowed myself one silent thought. Where, oh where, had she hidden her duty free cigarettes?

Anna's spirits lifted when I finally got her out of the hotel at 5pm. She found the view over the tranquil lake, with the warm light of the setting sun playing over them, very soothing. But then, when the backdrop of temple bells, gongs, cymbals and rolling drums announced the arrival of the evening *puja* ceremony, she had to retire to bed again.

Left to my own devices, I adjourned to the Sunset Cafe, just down from the Pushkar Palace hotel, to try out its brand-new range of ice-creams called DOLLOPS. Torn between a BIG LOP and a SNOW LOP FANTASY, I opted in the end for the LOP STICK CHOCO DASH and found it good.

What was not so good about the Sunset was the rat I spotted in the water well. 'Isn't that supplying all your guests with drinking water?' I asked the manager innocently. 'You see *nothing!'* he hissed at me and tried to shove a hundred rupee note into my hand.

The evening ended amusingly back at the Palace hotel, where I ordered a *thali* during a power cut. 'No curd, because fridge it is broke, my God!' exclaimed the waiter, dashing back and forth with a flickering candle. 'But tomorrow, *everything* is possible!'

I had a good chat with an English guy called Ben over my blacked-out *thali.* He stressed the importance of travelling alone in India – both for meeting people and for attuning to the ways, customs and people of this country at top speed. 'The reason so much more happens on your own is simple,' he concluded. 'You have to *make* it happen. And it won't happen half as easily when you have a boon companion – a permanent reminder of home – along for the ride.'

I winced at that. 'Tell me about it,' I thought.

*

I had just one problem with Pushkar. I couldn't really write about it. Well, I could, but I couldn't send any monied travellers there. First, there was the absence of quality accommodation – only one decent hotel, the Pushkar Palace – and then there was the food, or rather the lack of it.

'*The word cuisine doesn't really apply to Pushkar,*' I made a report into my Walkman. *'In fact, the word FOOD doesn't really apply to Pushkar, say many carnivores. This is a pure-veg holy town, with meat, alcohol, even eggs, off the menu. If there is one reason why the luxury groups stay away—apart from the ban on big 'mod-con' hotels—and why Pushkar will always remain the province of the budget backpacker, it is its limited selection of grub. Nearly every restaurant offers the same choice of bland, unexciting vegetarian fare—thalis, rice dishes and chips mainly—and even hardened hippies break after a week or two and scoot over to nearby Ajmer's Mansingh Hotel for a bottle of beer and a plate of chicken tikka. This said, if you are a devoted veggie, or are about to become one, Pushkar is just the place to be!'*

Pushkar was not the place for me to be the next day. Anna threw a wobbly over breakfast while I was chatting to, and taping, two medical students from the U.K. 'How am I going to deal with this?' I thought miserably. 'I *have* to keep interviewing people for my book. It's the only way it's going to stand out in the crowd.'

My mood improved as I strolled back into town. First, there was the ICE CRIME van I spotted in the market place. 'What's that?' I thought with a giggle. 'Death by lolly?' Then, opposite Gau Ghat, there was the shop to beat them all. It sold rubbers. 'Government price one rupee!' brayed the enthusiastic vendor. 'You can try them, no problem – one size fits all! This is nice things, with extra sensitivity! Try them on wife – and friends! Yes, condoms with perfumes!'

Proceeding on, I came to the Brahma Temple at the end of the market street. Some people thought this gaudy or 'Disneyish', but I liked the cheerful blue and pink colour scheme: it had a fresh, simple and clean appearance that I respected. And out the back – past the COW DONET money box – there was an incredible view straight onto the Great Thar Desert and the rolling dunes.

Having checked out all the 'hotels' in town – mainly ultra-basic cheapies for freaks and hippies – I returned to my own. And found Anna in the toilet again. 'I can't seem to hold these malaria tablets down,' she gurgled unhappily. 'Do you think I might have an allergic reaction to them?'

I mentally slapped myself. Of course. That had to be the problem. 'You're not taking any more of those,' I said, snatching the pack of little white pills from her. 'I've heard of malaria medication causing nausea and vomiting. Diarrhoea too. Hopefully, you'll feel better in the morning.'

Chapter 19

Night Train with Natalie

Anna did feel better the next morning, but not much. 'You go on by yourself for a bit,' she sighed after chanting about it. 'I've decided to stay and recuperate in Pushkar.'

'Are you sure?' I said, breathing an inner sigh of relief.

'Yes, quite sure,' she nodded weakly. 'I'm holding you back. You need to get on with your work without worrying about my health. Also, this hotel has a good toilet.'

Snatching up my bags, I leapt on the 9.30am departing bus to Ajmer with hardly enough time to confirm reunion arrangements with Anna next week in Jodhpur. I hoped that wouldn't be a problem.

'You are not a strange person!' a voice called up to me as the bus set in motion.

I looked out the window. It was Lalit Jain, aka Mr Bullshit. 'What?' I shouted down.

'Yus. You are not like a strange, you know?'

'Oh, riiiiight,' I said as the penny dropped. 'You mean "Don't be a stranger?"'

'Correct!' laughed Lalit. 'Don't be a strange-like!'

At Ajmer bus station, I marched up to the first Westerner I saw (the only one) and introduced myself. His name was David Bulley, a very pleasant chap from Clapham, London, and while he told me about Indian handicrafts I told him about my own time in Clapham (running a home for the elderly) and about Buddhism. We got along fine.

The six-hour drive west to Jodhpur was bumpy but very pleasant and we stopped at a couple of extremely colourful (red and yellow turbans bobbing all over the place) villages full of local farmers going off into the fields in smart little tractors. We were *very* popular here: people fell over themselves to see us. And David ate a bowl of white mush I wouldn't have fed to a pig. He loved it.

Around dusk, having seen nothing but arid wasteland and bare scrub for a while, we spotted the majestic fortress of Jodhpur rearing up like a stone leviathan atop a distant hill. 'Whoa, that's what I call a fort!' whistled David respectfully. 'It certainly is,' I agreed with a nod. 'And I've seen a few!'

In Jodhpur, I showed David to the New Tourist Hostel which had been recommended to me by Megan. Run by a tall, bespectacled Brahmin called Allen, it was apparently the 'cheap and best' place in town. It was also, we soon discovered, one of the friendliest. 'Welcome, my dear fatigued foreign friends!' cried Allen as we entered his establishment. 'How would you like your chocolate tea? Hot or cold?'

Chocolate tea was just one of Allen's armoury of interesting menu items. He also had MOUTHFUL NIBBLERS, VEGETABLE BULLET and BAKED WEAZLE. Unfortunately, since I had to be at Jodhpur railway station at 7.30pm sharp – when the ticket office opened for sleeper reservations to Jaiselmer – I barely had time to slurp my tea.

*

The only other Westerner on the night train to Jaiselmer was a young French girl. 'Hi,' I said as I moved up to join her. 'My name's Frank. What's yours?

At first I thought she hadn't heard me. Then she turned

around dreamily and said: 'Nathalie.'

'Natalie?'

'Yeth. Thath right,' she lisped, opening her mouth and pointing to her swollen tongue. 'I'm thorry, I juth have Thitha thident out.'

'Thitha thident?'

She stuck three fingers in the air to indicate a three-pronged fork.

'Oh, you mean a *Shiva trident?'* I said as light dawned. 'What on Earth made you stick that in your tongue?'

Natalie's eyes rolled at the effort of having to continue the conversation. Then, with several more hand gestures thrown in, she told me her story. 'Thomeone tell me Thitha thident in tongue is good luck, tho I let him do it. But then I meet hanthome Italian guy in Jaipur and he arthk me to…erm…"go down on him". What happen next ith not good luck. I make holth in hith penith.'

'Holth? Penith? You mean holes in his penis?'

'Yeth. Big holth. He muth go to hoth'pital.'

'Ouch,' I exclaimed. 'Is he okay?'

'Yeth,' she said with a wry smile. 'But I do not think he will be having th'ex for a very long time.'

Chapter 20

Camels at Dawn

I had my best sleep on a train so far – a solid six hours. And we drew into Jaiselmer unexpectedly early, at 7.30am. Leaning out of a window, coughing through the soot and the smoke of the engine, I rubbed my eyes. Emerging from the empty wilderness, the towering hilltop fort suddenly loomed up out of nowhere – a fantastic mirage straight out of the Arabian Nights.

But Jaiselmer was not my priority. 'The real Jaiselmer is no longer in the small town in the fort,' Megan's words came back to me, 'but out in the desert villages. If you want to go off the beaten track and make your guidebook different, Frank, you should try and get out to Khuri.'

I had heard a lot about Khuri. For the past 12 or so years, Western tourists had made the arduous trip out to Jaiselmer with one main objective – to do the big camel trek into the Great Thar Desert. But the best part of the desert, the rolling sand dunes, didn't actually appear till some 40 kilometres *out* of Jaiselmer. 'All we saw for two days,' commented one disillusioned traveller, 'were telegraph poles, dusty highways full of army trucks, and fizzy drink vendors. We didn't get a sniff of a sand dune, just bare and empty scrubland.'

Khuri was different. According to all reports, it was *the* place to go to see white, rolling dunes – mile upon mile of them, for as far as the eye could see. It was also the gateway to the real Rajput people, folklore and customs and marked the culmination of many travellers' Rajasthani journey.

But getting there wasn't easy. First off, the guy who generally met travellers at Jaiselmer's first fort gate – Bhagwan Singh – wasn't there. It was the end of his 'tourist season' and he had retired to his village. Second, Natalie decided – on an impulse – to join me. I wasn't sure about this unexpected trail buddy, but it turned out okay. It later transpired that Khuri was not a place to go on your own – unless you enjoyed sand and camels as your only company.

The third obstacle was the worst. Grabbing two tiny seats in the 10am bus to Khuri, we waited for an hour until it became so impossibly crowded that there was little point hanging around anymore. So it left, at 11am. There ensued a madcap, rolling adventure down a dusty highway into the heart of the Great Indian Desert, with everybody with any sense transferring from the hot interior of the bus to the roof. 'This is so *cool'* I shouted to Natalie as the fierce desert wind buffeted my weathered brow. 'Yeth,' she lisped happily. 'Ikth's tho exthiting!'

An hour and a half later, and having travelled 45 kilometres south-west of Jaiselmer, we piled off the bus…and into the waiting arms of Bhagwan Singh. 'Ah, you are the world-famous journalist!' said the big, bearded man, pumping my hand furiously. 'My brother, Tane, come quick by motorbike – tell me the news!'

'I don't know about world famous,' I said with a smile. 'But I guess a few people know me in Clapham. So, what can you tell me about Khuri?'

'Here in Khuri we are not out to exploit tourists', said Bhagwan, guiding us slowly to the village. 'We want them to see the real way of the desert. And we are determined to keep our traditional customs and values, even if this means living somewhat in the past with simple means and few luxuries. Visitors who do not respect our culture, or who press business on us, we turn away.'

I was impressed by Bhagwan. He was a surprisingly young, sophisticated and educated Rajput. As for his mother, Mama Singh, she was even more of a revelation. Bedecked in jewellery and grinning from ear to ear, she couldn't have been more welcoming. 'Sit! Sit!' she commanded as a huge lunch of varied breads, chutneys and vegetarian dishes came into view. 'You must eat!'

Over the next hour or so, I learnt all about Khuri. It was the central village of about 100 smaller settlements ruled by the Rajput Sodhas, a 'fire caste' who hailed their origin from a mythological hero called Parma. There were about 2000 inhabitants, though about half of these were wandering nomads who travelled far afield in search of water and fodder for their cattle. Noble, dignified Father Singh – who appeared briefly – was the head man, but the real power behind the throne was Mama Singh. 'You eat more!' came another command from this large, charismatic lady. 'You have too little body!'

Stuffed to the gills, Natalie and I were next shown around the village – a charming, modest collection of small mud-and-stone beehive dwellings (many painted with Aztec-like patterns by the women), interspersed with a few wicker cattle pens. Everywhere we went, we were followed by smiling, welcoming children and invited to 'take tea' in family homes. 'Blimey,' I thought. 'I feel like Fletcher Christian landing on Tahiti. These people are really pleased to see us!'

At sunset, we climbed to the roof of the 'hospitality' building and watched the evening sky turn deep, silky velvet-blue and the thin cloud tissue burn a vivid rose-pink before fading suddenly into darkness. Night fell very quickly and there was no electricity, only oil-lamps. The evening was spent with Bhagwan Singh and his chums in the courtyard below, supping the desert 'country wine' and listening to the low, atmospheric women's songs and village drums. Then, since the huts allocated to us were too hot to sleep in, beds were made up for us outside and we drifted off to sleep under a canopy of glittering stars.

*

I wasn't sure I wanted to do a two-day camel trek across a wide, open desert in 40 degrees of heat. It sounded jolly uncomfortable. On the other hand, this would be a big coup for me – even Lonely Planet hadn't covered it yet. Added to which, the Sodha family had been so effusive in their welcome and so keen for me to write them up. It seemed impolite to say 'No.'

After a blowout breakfast Natalie and I were introduced to our camel-drivers: two wiry, grinning, orange-turbaned men called Gamera Singh and Ismarom. Both guides spoke better camel than English and they were obsessed with Natalie's name. Mounting the heavy camels and setting off at a stately gait out of the village, they began experimenting with that name, loudly and repeatedly. It went on for hours. In between this, Ismarom revealed himself a demon masseur. Both off and on the camel, he was pummelling away on our backs, necks, heads, and eventually, buttocks and legs. By the evening, poor Natalie was a tenderised jelly.

We rode for about two hours – stopping at the most attractive dunes – then came to rest at another village. The head-man here was *another* Bhagwan Singh: a hook-nosed, keen-eyed, but generally crazy Rajput who – once the initial reserve was gone – warmed to me to such an extent that I was soon his 'brother'. Poor Natalie. She went to sleep in the large hospitality hut at 11am with just three people around her. When she woke an hour later, no less than 32 pairs of curious eyes were staring at her. Practically the whole extended family had come in to escape from the heat and to meet us.

There followed four of the weirdest and most entertaining

hours of my life – exchanging gifts, clothes and pleasantries, listening to the popular tongue-twisting traditional prayer-songs (only successful if accomplished in a single breath), and photographing Rajput elders in heritage dress and Vaselined curling moustaches, all the while being fanned by a friendly punkah wallah wearing a pair of disintegrating desert slippers. At one point, Bhagwan Singh, who had never seen a camera before, grabbed mine and tried to take a photograph. The flash went, he leapt back in fright and amazement, and all the rest of the family clapped and laughed and went 'WAAAHH!'

At 4pm, with the heat less intense, we moved on again. The vista was a silent, empty, yellow-white wasteland of rolling sands, populated only by scrub, hole-pitted warrens occupied by tiny, scurrying desert rats, a few berry trees (the camels loved those) and the occasional bouncing white-bummed deer. By 6pm, however, my own bum was killing me and I went into a sulk. 'When we stop?' I grumbled to Ismarom. 'Too much pain!' This was his cue to fling me on the ground and pummel my buttocks again. 'Soon! Soon!' he chuckled, but he was lying. It was a long hour later before we reached our resting point for the night and in all that time tears flowed freely down my cheeks.

Evening *gongyo*, performed to the gathering gloom of the dusk, restored my humour. 'Okay,' I thought. 'I'm sitting on a raised sand dune in the middle of nowhere with a sore bum. But there is one compensation. That village I gave all my fags, postcards and English coins to earlier gifted *me* two bottles of Panther Triple X army issue rum.'

It was at this point that Natalie revealed herself to be a closet alcoholic. 'Super strong!' Ismarom said approvingly as I brought forth my largesse. 'You will like!' Well, Natalie liked alright. She guzzled a whole bottle without blinking. And turned from a quiet, demure young hippy with hardly anything to say into a loud, drunken harpy with a mouth like a drain. 'Thuck you all!' she slurred as she began dancing around the camp fire. 'I'm having the beth thucking time of my life!'

The camel drivers clapped in appreciation. 'Atlee good!' said Gamera Singh.

'I love Italy!' chipped in Ismarom.

'It's not Atlee or Italy,' I said between gritted teeth. 'For the last time, it's Natalie.'

'Thuck,' said Gamera Singh.

'Naughty very funny,' said Ismarom. 'Why she no have husband?'

Just then, as Natalie ran out of dance moves and slumped to the ground, a small, white scorpion ran over her hand and all hell broke loose.

'Thucketythuckthuck*thuck!*' she screamed, lurching to her feet again. 'I thucking *hate* thorpionths!'

'OhmyGod!' I squealed as the scuttling creature made a beeline for me. 'So do I!'

Our camel drivers found our discomfiture highly amusing. 'Why worry?' laughed Gamera Singh, flicking it away with a stick. 'If you are bitten, we take you to next village – they will chant a mantra over you!'

'How comforting', I thought as I reached for the other bottle of rum. 'I'm getting trollied.'

I woke at 4am with a hangover and took ages to get to sleep again. Our camp was surrounded by baying dogs, the fire had gone out, the mosquitoes had arrived, and so had the white ants. All the insect life of the desert seemed to be queuing up to have a nibble. But the sky was a real delight: all the stars were out and as I looked up at this sparkling array, I smiled in recognition. It was a carbon-copy of the Mirror Palace's ceiling in Jaipur's Amber Fort.

The sunrise, like the sunset, was another desert spectacle. It heralded the arrival of a huge breakfast, cooked by the drivers, and a glorious pot of steaming cardamom tea. 'How do you feel this morning?' I asked Natalie as we watched Gamara Singh patting more *rotis* into shape, ready for the frying pan. 'Don't arsthk,' she groaned. 'My head hurth.'

I didn't have the heart to tell her there were four more hours on a camel coming up.

Fortunately, we returned to Khuri at 11.30am – much earlier than expected. By the time we got back, however, I had snapped two sets of leather stirrups just standing up in the saddle to give my rear end some relief. Forget the romance of *Lawrence of Arabia* – when those camels broke into a bum-crunching canter it was like the most excruciating kind of Chinese torture.

But all in all, it had been a wonderful experience. After a much-needed cold shower, Mama Singh treated us to a special lunch and as many liquid refreshments as we could handle. Then the whole Sodha family crowded around to make their farewells and to see us safely onto the 4.30pm bus back to Jaiselmer. I would remember their hospitality for years to come.

Chapter 21

The Great Indian Bustard of Jaiselmer

Jaiselmer was a bit of a comedown after the desert. We missed the easy-going, relaxed, quiet serenity of Khuri, and the noise, dust, and crowds of the city instantly depressed us. Fortunately, Bhagwan Singh had recommended a good hotel – the Hotel Pleasure just inside the city gate – which *was* a pleasure. The friendly manager, Didi, was a positive mine of useful information. So was another friend of Bhagwan's, Rajeev, who turned up to give us a free tour – lasting the whole day – right round town.

Thanks to these two guys, and together with my own observations, I was able to compile a report for Paula in double-quick time:

Situated about 400 miles due west of Pushkar, right on the Pakistan border, Jaiselmer is a beautiful old frontier town – still full of character and characters – dating back to the 12th century. All the action takes place within the huge yellow-sandstone fort, perched on a high hill, which encloses the town and which looks out onto the bare Thar Desert for miles in all directions. This fort, ringed by 6 kilometres of battlements and fortified walls, was built to last and it repelled all invaders, even including the Persian Mughals. It also lay directly on the ancient camel caravan routes leading out to Sind (present-day Pakistan), which brought its Jain merchants and bankers great power and wealth between the 14th and 16th centuries.

The town itself is small and friendly, full of winding streets and dark little alleyways, and there's hardly ever more than a handful of westerners around. There's lots of cheap cafes in Jaiselmer, most of them offering basic backpacker fare like VEGEMITE TOST, BROWN BRAID, and CHEE'S BALL. Others, like the rooftop Treat restaurant, offer '108 items of traditional Rajasthani food', but the service tends to be slow. Why? Well, according to the menu, SHORT TIME DESTROYED THE COOKING. Just below the Treat is a famous sign, with an arrow pointing out to the empty desert, which reads:

SEE THE GOLDEN DESERTED BED OF JAISELMER!

DESERTED MEALS ON THE ROOF!

TOURISTICK AND NON-TOURISTICK!

Jaiselmer's principal attraction is its very real feel of antiquity—the mediaeval town is still pretty feudal, and grizzled Rajasthanis still prowl the streets with bandoliers and ancient weapons strapped to their chest...'

What *was* a bandolier, Natalie interrupted excitedly, and where could she buy one? When I explained that bandoliers were cartridge belts for muskets—primitive muskets with very unstable firing pins – I thought she would go off the idea, but no, it just made her more determined. Now she wanted a bandolier *and* a musket. Back at the Pleasure, she asked a puzzled Didi where the nearest bandolier shop was. There wasn't one of course, so she started stalking elderly Rajputs in the street, just in case she could buy an ancient weapon on the cheap. It was only when I firmly told her that a musket would never be allowed on the plane home—probably a bandolier also—that she reluctantly backed off.

To distract her, I took her down to the Gadisar Tank, just

below the city walls. This was the large natural oasis which lured the Bhati prince Jaisal to the site 800 years ago, and which was the city's main source of water until the recent droughts. That afternoon, we found it just a shallow depression in the surrounding desert, strewn with bleached cenotaphs. Disappointed, I tried to interest Natalie in the splendid views of the battlemented fort from atop the Krishna temple, and the beautiful arched gateway said to have been erected by the famous prostitute Tilo, but she wasn't impressed. She only perked up when we paid a visit to Gadisar's quaint little Folklore Museum and she found a copy of a local guidebook.

'Look here!' she chuckled happily. 'It telth you all about the Great Indian Buthtard of Jaithelmer!'

'What's the Great Indian Bustard of Jaiselmer?'

'I'm *very* glad you arthked me that. Read thith!'

'It is a beautiful and extremely popular bird found over area in Jaiselmer,' I read over her shoulder. *'It attains the height of 2 to 3 feet. Its neck is long like that of a camel. Which it moves side ways while walking. Its eyes shine like the eyes of a deer. Its voice is very sweet. It feeds on gravel. At the approach of the men it takes to flight. It's a very scarce bird found in the world.'*

We gazed dumbfounded at the picture of the Bustard in the book. It seemed to be a composite of three separate birds pasted unevenly together—the head of a seagull, the body of a chicken, and the spindly legs of a pigeon. This was one rare bustard indeed, never to have been photographed in its entirety.

The next morning, I was surprised to find Didi laid low by flu. Well, he was only laid low for intermittent periods. He kept rising from his sick-bed to mope and moan restlessly round the lodge, and to howl like a distressed calf. He even managed to climb across the roof to adjoining houses to show his neighbours how sick he was.

At the bottom of the fort, I tried to put through a call to my mother in London from the INTERNATIONAL FRUNK PHONE SERVICE. I wanted to make sure she had some frankfurters and chips on hand when I got home in a couple of weeks. But half an hour later, despite the sign outside saying DIAL AND TALK FOREIGN AT ONCE, I had got precisely nowhere. Just as I began muttering expletives at the silent telephone receiver, the guy at reception leant over and said: 'Sir, if you get used to things not being prompt, this is the first step to loving India!'

I took it easy the rest of the day. That Khuri trek had really taken it out of me. But I did struggle up to the fort ramparts to visit the Hotel Paradise, which Rajeev had recommended as the 'cheap and best' place to stay in Jaiselmer. He was not wrong. For once, the self-advertisement – ROYAL BALCONIES ROOMS WITH TOILET AND NICE VIEW, GIVES THE FEELINGS TO OUR CUSTOMERS AS BEING THE MOST LUCKY – was spot on. Some of the rooms had spectacular views over the town and desert, and there was even a chilled beer service!

At 9pm I travelled with Natalie to the rail station for the night train to Jodhpur, arriving just in time for a dust storm which swept with blinding force over the platforms. Our eyes streamed as we scanned the station for somewhere to hide. Then, just as I thought we would suffocate, two young lads beckoned us into the only chai shop in sight and treated us to loads of free tea. Everyone else on the platforms – except a parasitical German called Jochen who contrived to join us – choked half to death. I left Jaiselmer overwhelmed by the hospitality of the people: so charming, warm and genuinely friendly. The tea boys even left their urn to come and wave us off.

Jochen turned out to be a right pain in the ass. Since Natalie had attracted him (he knew her faintly from Pushkar) I tried to switch off and leave him to her. But it wasn't easy. His whole conversation centred around drugs and dubious wheelings and dealings. 'Can we talk about something else?' I suggested at one point, but he wasn't listening. Jochen, in fact, was incapable of listening to anything. Compulsively loquacious and oozing nervous energy, he reminded me of a highly-strung, insensitive puppy-dog. 'Can you stop doing that?' I said irritatedly as he delved yet again into my water and oranges. 'You've got supplies of your own!' But once again, Jochen wasn't listening. Then came the final straw – he brushed a cloud of dust off his top bunk into my face. 'Be more careful!' I hissed at him, and he just giggled. This was my cue to abandon my Buddhist principles and go for his throat. He was much quieter after that.

Chapter 22

Maharajah Massage

Back in Jodhpur at 6.30am, I politely but firmly dissuaded Jochen from following me to my hotel. Natalie, however, had to come. 'I try to get Railway Retiring room,' she said. 'But they wouldn't thore (*store) my ruckthack without a lock. How do you lock a ruckthack?'

It was good to be back with the charming, erudite Allen at the New Tourist Hostel. He had saved me his very best room – a rather dusty and simple effort, but with a clean bathroom attached – and had a pot of chocolate tea on the go as soon as we arrived. 'You must drink quick!' he encouraged us. 'You will need all strength for fort!'

Jodhpur Fort was a real revelation. The biggest and best in India, I'll be bound. And Allen was right – the crippling 30-minute climb to the top was no picnic. 'No wonder the place was never captured,' I puffed to Natalie as we reached our goal. 'Any prospective invader must have been knackered by the time they got up here!'

The central feature of the fort was its magnificent City Palace Museum. Never before had I seen so much opulence, expert craftsmanship and royal finery concentrated in one building. Starting with the chamber full of baby-carriages (home of many fledgling Maharajahs), moving on to the haveli-type ladies' quarters with their stone-carved balconies, we passed through a whole series of mini-palaces and courtyards to reach the sumptuous royal bedroom with its truly amazing centrepiece – the vast bed where the Maharajah 'entertained' his 35 wives.

What surprised me, looking around, was that Natalie and I seemed to be the only foreign visitors. Then I remembered Megan's words: 'Jodhpur may be the largest city in Rajasthan, but it is curiously unappreciated. Most travellers use it as a jumping-off point to Jaiselmer (west), Udaipur (south) and Jaipur (east). This may have something to do with the heat – pretty severe, except from December to February – but I think it's a lot to do with the hassle factor. Women travellers have a particularly hard time here, and everybody is plagued by kids chanting "Wottis your nem?" and begging school pens.'

Certain sections of the fort – notably the ladies' quarters inside the museum – provided fine views down over the Brahmin quarter of town, which was painted bright blue in honour of Lord Krishna. To see all this royal blue to best advantage, however, we had to head out of the museum and up to the fort ramparts. Looking down over the neat, serried ranks of brilliant-blue Brahmin houses, we could see why Jodhpur was termed the 'blue city' of Rajasthan, just as Jaipur and Jaiselmer were called the 'pink' and 'amber' cities respectively.

A short rickshaw ride south took us down from the fort through the old city market, a teeming thoroughfare of narrow, winding lanes crammed with bicycles, carts, cows and camels. What we didn't see here wasn't worth mentioning – it was a wild, colourful potpourri of street tailors, candle-makers, incense sellers, sugar-cane presses, glass and lantern shops, all casually observed by old men sitting in doorways propped on silver-topped cane sticks. At one point we got stuck in the narrow-lane traffic and watched young lads playing games with live rats – they were throwing them back and forth, the aim being to catch them by the tail, losers got bitten. 'Oh my God!' came a shriek from a neighbouring rickshaw when a flying rodent landed in it.

Jodhpur was famous for its *makhania* lassis, a rich, creamy drink made with cow's milk, butterballs, cardamom and ice. 'Abthulety delithuth!' said Natalie, stopping to glug down a glass of the stuff. 'Absolutely yuk!' I gagged in violent disagreement.

Jodhpur was also famous for its strange Government Museum at the north-eastern end of the Umaid Public Gardens. DOGS AND HOBNAIL BOOTS NOT ALLOWED warned the sign at the entrance, but we never found out why. All there was inside, apart from some nice porcelain and pottery pieces, was a giant model ear, an odd montage of human entrails, a boil-ridden child, and a ghastly flayed traffic policeman. 'Watch your step,' I warned Natalie as we picked our way out again via a dark, dank tunnel. 'I think I just tripped over a stuffed crocodile.'

At 6pm, I waved Natalie off on a night bus to Delhi and returned to Allen's place to wait for Anna. Yes, a whole week had passed since I had left my loved one latched to a toilet in Pushkar. I wondered how she had got on.

It was 8.15pm, much later than expected, that Anna finally arrived. Her dark, bouncy hair was streaked with grime and there was a look of tired desperation on her face.

'All the rickshaw drivers were scared of me,' she said without any preamble. 'This silly Western woman obviously very stressed out and haggard and thin. I got one eventually but he had no idea of where to take me since you were in a rush to reach Jaiselmer and just threw a name at me. How was I to know it was the New Tourist Hostel and not the Tourist Hotel? Whatever, he drove me first to a brothel and then to a gambling den before we chanced on the hole in the wall which just happened to be where you were staying.'

My reply was not a study in tact. 'Good Lord,' I said. 'Where's your bum gone?'

'It's gone where the rest of me has gone,' said Anna rather snippily. 'I only started holding food down again two days ago. And you could at least give me a hug. Aren't you pleased to see me?

My arms wrapped around her much diminished contours. 'Of course I am,' I mumbled in reply. 'And I'm so glad you made it. I was getting really worried about you.'

Her look told me everything. She wasn't convinced.

*

That night I racked my brains trying to think of a way to cheer Anna up. Then I had it. She liked a good massage.

'Do you know where I might find a good masseur here in Jodhpur?' I asked Allen over breakfast.

'Oh yes,' he said, pointing at the gnarled old figure shambling around the grounds with a broom. 'You are in luck. This man, he is personal massage man for Maharajah of Jodhpur!'

'Really?' I replied, eyeing the gap-toothed ancient distrustfully. 'What's he doing here?'

'He work for me. He no work for Maharajah for ten years.'

'Well, do you think you can persuade him to come out of retirement? I could really use a good massage guy right now.'

Allan nodded, and went over to have a word with his sweeper.

'It is good. He can come your room right now.'

Rubbing my hands together with suppressed glee, I woke

Anna up and gave her the good news. 'I'll leave you alone for a bit,' I told her. 'You're about the have the best massage of your life!'

All was quiet for an hour while I took some notes in the courtyard, and then there was a loud scream.

'I don't believe it!' said Anna, bursting out of the room with just a towel clasped around her. 'I just woke up and that guy was massaging my tits!'

'What do you mean you just woke up? Did he put you to sleep?'

'Yes, he did. He was doing my back and I dropped off. He must have turned me around!'

Well, I wasn't having that. I marched over to Allen's office to make a complaint.

'You told me this was best massage man in Jodhpur!' I accosted him. 'What is he doing massaging my girlfriend's breasts?'

Allan went deathly pale.

'He is massaging your girlfriend?' he said in shock. 'I thought he was massaging *you*. This man, he has never touched a Western woman before!'

In between running around town gathering information – not helped by the tourist officer taking a marathon three-and-a-half hour 'lunch break' – I tried to book sleeper berths for the night train to Udaipur. 'Why you no take bus?' said Allen. 'Bus is good. It stop midway for beautiful temple of Ranakpur.' I shook my head. 'Thanks, but no thanks. A friend of mine arrived there at some big Jain festival, got dragged off the bus by a sea of pilgrims, and was force-fed and treated like everyone's long-lost brother for three whole days. That's not happening to me.'

In retrospect, I should have listened to Allen. Down at the

railway station, I fell into the clutches of a wily old codger called Dr Subthia who got me train tickets immediately but who held off on the actual sleeper reservations. I listened to him drone on for a while in the upstairs railway canteen, then went back to Allen's where I learnt that he was a notorious cheat – one to be avoided at all costs. 'Go to Northern Railway Divisional Superintendent's office,' suggested Allen. 'He will give you confirmed reservations, sure!'

Allen was right. An hour later, having bid him and his calm oasis of a guest house a fond farewell, I was back at the railway station with Anna, clutching two precious sleeper reservations. 'This is no good!' said a wildly protesting Dr Subthia as he descended upon us. 'I get you V.I.P. tourist quota reservations!'

I shot him a look of massive no confidence. 'Yes, but at what price? Go away. You are bad man.'

Dr Subthia was, however, not in a listening mood. He ranted on and on until, quite unexpectedly, Anna started chanting hard at him…in the middle of a crowded platform.

'Now repeat after me,' she said when he finally fell silent. 'Nam-myoho-renge-kyo. Nam-myoho-renge-kyo. It will make you happy.'

I looked at Anna with a new respect. Why hadn't I thought of that?

It worked too. After mumbling a few mantras along with her the errant doctor slunk away, hopefully never to prey on innocent tourists again.

Chapter 23

Hello, Mr James Bond. Where is your Horse?

I was looking forward to sharing Udaipur with Anna. I had had such a good time here last year with my Australian friend, Jenny. Surely this beautiful 'Venice of the East' – with its fairy-tale lakes and palaces – would enchant her too.

'What do you want to see first?' I asked as we woke on the train and enjoyed the rest of our delicious water melon for breakfast. 'There's a *lot* on offer.'

Anna shot me a shy smile from her bottom bunk. 'Well, I'd love to see the City Palace, of course. Oh, and that quaint "Science Museum" with its sea monsters in milk bottles and the skeleton in a sari sounds fun.'

But once again she was plagued by ill luck. Having arrived in Udaipur and checked into the much-recommended Hotel Sagar overlooking Fateh Sagar Lake, we learnt that both the City Palace and the Science Museum were closed. 'Today not good day,' mumbled the hotel manager. 'All government building closed for holiday.'

It wasn't a lucky day for me either. The tourist office was dour and unhelpful, and when I went to interview the best guide in town – my old friend Bhaji at the Jagat Niwas hotel in Lake Palace Rd – my Walkman seized up. Frustrated and tired, we returned to our hotel to find all sorts of loud noise and music going on, and the place was full of flies. 'Today is a plastic spider day,' I informed Anna miserably. 'Let's go to bed early.'

*

An early night led to us waking at dawn. Which in turn meant we couldn't find anywhere to have breakfast. 'Let's try the Jagat Niwas hotel,' I suggested. 'I've fixed my Walkman and want to have another bash at interviewing Bhaji. He's "Mr Memory" round here and knows everything there is to know about Udaipur and its environs.'

But the Jagat Niwas was dead as a dodo. Only one sleepy waiter attended our persistent ringing of the reception bell. 'What you want?' he yawned. 'We want breakfast,' we replied. 'Okay,' he said and sloped off to have it made. A long 20 minutes later, he shuffled back with two plates, but there was a problem. Anna's scrambled eggs had arrived in boiled form. 'When you scrambled those eggs,' she informed the waiter. 'You forgot to take the shells off.' The waiter giggled. 'Can I have another one?' asked Anna. 'This time without the protective covering?' The waiter giggled again. 'So sorry,' he said. 'Big cook come, little cook go.'

Anna and I exchanged a look of consternation. Was he mad?

'Big cook come soon from Lake Palace hotel,' a voice came from behind us. 'You wait.'

We turned to find Raja, the hotel manager, who had just surfaced nursing a hangover. Even at this early time of the morning, Raja was the very epitome of Rajput style and dash. With his meticulously clipped moustache, designer T-shirt, and gold medallion he looked like a Bollywood movie star. 'Only *big* cook make scrambled egg,' he explained. 'Present cook no allow.'

Well, that made sense. We thanked him, left him a note for

Bhaji, and began to peel our eggs.

Back at the Hotel Sagar, Anna had an argument with young Kanti, the room boy, about *dhobi* (laundry). He had managed to stain all her white shirts purple. Then she asked for a ladies' bicycle to go touring on, but nobody had one. 'These men's bikes are too big for me!' she said with a peep in her voice. 'I'm only a wee, small person!'

Just then, an auto-rickshaw drew up. 'Hello, Mr James Bond!' chirruped the grinning driver. 'Where is your horse?'

'What's he talking about?' said Anna, her anger defused by this curious greeting.

I laughed. 'Oh, you don't know, do you? A lot of the film *Octopussy* was filmed here in Udaipur. They call *every* Westerner James Bond. There's even a café in town, the Mayur, which screens it every night. I asked the owner what he thought of it last year, and he said "When I watch it now, I am getting boring."'

The rickshaw driver's name was Ram, and he took us all around Udaipur – first to a charming puppet show at Bhartiya Lok Kala Mandal, then to the picturesque gardens of Sahelion-ki-Bari, then to the pretty island garden of Nehru Park shimmering in the middle of Fateh Sagar Lake, and finally to Udaipur's biggest and best temple – the Jagdish Temple – where we were lucky enough to find local ladies practising prayer-songs and traditional hymns, accompanied by lively temple musicians.

The highlight of the day, however, was the ultra-romantic Lake Palace Hotel on Jag Niwas island. Built around 1740 as a summer palace for the Maharana, it was a poem in white marble – sitting on calm Pichola Lake like an iced wedding cake on a tray of glass. 'Ooh, I like this,' said Anna as our little boat chugged out to the island. 'Why can't we stay here for a night?' I rolled my eyes. 'Because we'd be washing dishes for a month, that's why. The cheapest rooms are about fifty quid!'

Settling instead for a sunset drink on the hotel veranda – Anna sipping on a cool cocktail, me swigging an iced 'deluxe' beer – we watched the bird-scarers on the top terraces lassoo pigeons (they spoilt the paintwork) and waited for the still waters of the lake to turn first coppery-yellow, then a fiery blood-red. After dusk – a final nice touch – flocks of giant fruit bats swept over the lake. It was like another scene out of Hitchcock's *The Birds.*

Returned to land, we raced back to the Jagat Niwas hotel for my proposed meeting with Bhaji at 8pm. 'I hope he got my note,' I told Anna. 'Otherwise, I'm screwed.' But I needn't have worried. Bhaji was waiting for us at reception and over the next hour or two, with my whirring little Walkman drinking in his every word, I got the best and most informed exposition of Udaipur – and of Indian customs, social life, and religion – possible. 'Ah, you are Buddhist,' he declared when we revealed our religion. 'Then you must understand why India is country of extremes, why it has no middle-range hotel or middle range anything. It lose the Middle Way when it turn its back on Buddhism.'

This was unusually profound for a fairly low caste Indian and with mixed curiosity and respect we told him so.

'I am also Buddhist,' he confessed with a smile. 'Have you heard of Nam-myoho-renge-kyo?'

Chapter 24

Crash and Burn in Mount Abu

While I ate an awful 'sweet' at a roadside *dhaba*, Anna flew into a fit on the 'luxury' bus taking us on to Mount Abu. This bus was a real rip-off – no reclining seats, all windows either cracked or jammed closed, and our promised 'front' seats turned out to be at the back.

Our host for this particular trip was an ebullient young man in a ragged woolly jumper called Dinesh. Dinesh was the conductor on this bus and he tried to placate Anna by inviting her to sleep on his palette up in the driver's cockpit. 'Sleep?' raged Anna, her teeth rattling in her head. 'This bus is like the Deadwood Stage – I've never been on such a bumpy road in my life!'

Still keen to please, Dinesh next put on a video. This depicted a fat Indian swain singing 'Humdrum Baby' to a tree, and even Dinesh couldn't take it. He asked us for some Western music instead, so I handed him a tape entitled 'Now that's what I call Music, Volume Two.' Twenty seconds into Chaka Khan, the driver got bored and turned it off.

'Where's my music?' I complained.

'Not available,' shrugged Dinesh.

I promptly re-entitled my tape 'Now that's what I call Not Available.'

Minutes later, the bus was stormed by 24 lager louts who turned out to be law students on a day out. Eight of them piled into the front cabin and one of them tried to sit on the driver's lap while he was going at 60 miles an hour. The bus screeched to a halt – to discuss the backhander they had to pay the driver in lieu of a recorded fare – and then it set off again.

At this point, Dinesh remembered my request for alcohol and the bus took a 20 kilometre detour to a small village in the middle of nowhere with a blue-grilled 'English Wine' shop. The shop was shut, but I only had ten seconds to wait before a ragged figure loomed out of the shadows with a key.

'You are wanting *bonking?'* it enquired.

'I'm not sure I have time for sexual favours,' I nervously replied. 'Haven't you got any rum?'

'Yes, *bonking!*' the figure insisted and stuffed an opaque bottle in my hands. 'This is *Bon King* – number one selling rum!'

Mount Abu was a real surprise: nothing like what I'd expected. Instead of a stony, craggy retreat of Jain monks, it was a jolly little place of ice-cream parlours, pony rides, omelette stalls, 'fun' shops, and (the main feature) honeymooning Indian couples.

Off the bus, another surprise, we were surrounded by young lads wanting to wheel our luggage to our hotel in small brightly-coloured baby prams.

'Where you go?' they chorused.

'Here,' I replied. Jessica in Madras had prepared me for this assault. She had even given me her party piece.

'Where you go?' said the pram-boys again.

'Here. I stay here.'

Stymied, they looked at each other, nodded, and went off. Then they tried everyone else and came back to us for a second chance. We ended up with pram-boy Ram. Ram's first gambit was: 'Savera Palace-number-one-hotel-where-you-go?' To which I replied: 'Don't know. Staying here. Waiting.' Ram suggested that we 'wait Savera Palace'. I suggested we wait Hotel Hilltone (Jessica's choice), but Ram didn't want to go there. He curled his lip, bared his teeth, and uttered the cryptic phrase 'One per cent.' Whether this referred to the status of Hotel Hilltone or to the negligible amount of commission he could expect for taking us there, we never discovered. We asked him what 'One per cent' meant, and he just said he was 'not fully English'.

The Hotel Hilltone, when we finally got there, was a real find. Refreshingly quiet (i.e. no post-nuptial goings on next door), it had lovely gardens, good room service, smart, courteous staff, nice restaurant, even a 'complimentary shoeshine'. It was a lot better than the Savera Palace with its ethnic cave-décor rooms, roller-skating rink, steam bath (HOT WATER PUDLE), and blaring videos in the TV lounge.

I don't know what it was, whether the sudden change in temperature – Abu was a good 20 degrees cooler than Udaipur – or the strain of constant travel for nearly two months, but I suddenly felt like I'd been hit by a sledgehammer. While Anna went into town to sample Abu's trademark ginger tea, I passed out on the bed and slept for a solid 12 hours. 'I've really got to slow down,' I vaguely thought as I lost consciousness. 'Otherwise, I'll crash and burn.'

*

Slowing down was, however, not an option. It was now March 20th, I only had 11 days left in the country, and there was so much left to do! If I stayed on that bed, as every nerve of my body was screaming at me, I would never get off it. 'Now I know how you must have been feeling,' I groaned to Anna as we took the morning tour of Abu by mini-bus. 'I can barely move my legs.' Anna shot me a perky look of *schadenfreude.* 'Well, you might have to, Frank. I hear there's a lot of climbing coming up!'

She wasn't joking. Every place the bus stopped, and there were quite a few, involved long climbs up hundreds of steps. 'I want to die,' I complained as I dragged my weary bones to the final stop, the famous Jain temples at Dilwara. 'You'll have to bring me down by mule.'

But then I entered the large complex and my complaints melted away. Five magnificent temples stretched before me – two of them, the Vimal Vasahi and the Luna Vasahi, representing the finest Jain architecture in India. I was particularly struck by the Luna Vasahi. Built in 1231 and dedicated to the 22nd *Tirthankar* (Jain saint) Neminath, this filigree fantasy temple – with its translucent lotuses dripping from the porch dome, its glorious overhead panels of deities and attendants, its high-towered prayer hall, and its massive statue of Neminath – were all carved from a single massive block of Macrana marble.

'Stunning, isn't it?' I turned to remark to Anna. 'I hear that each worker was paid in solid gold, and in direct proportion to the weight of marble covered.'

But Anna wasn't there. She was back at the entrance being quizzed by a security guard. He was pointing at a sign saying WOMEN ON THEIR MONTHLY COURSE MUST NOT ENTER – THOSE WHO DO MAY SUFFER! Anna was hopping up and down with rage at this. 'How do you know if I am or if I'm not?' she protested. 'Just let me in!' The guard shook his head. 'I have much practice in this thing,' he said with finality. 'I see it in your eyes.'

'That was a shame,' I told Anna as I dragged her, still wildly protesting, away. 'You should have worn sunglasses.'

Back in town, Anna dragged me – lethargic and over-tired – off to Nakki Lake. Here, after failing to get anywhere in a paddle boat with tiny paddles we had a good time in a proper rowing boat where I managed to row myself back into a good mood. Falling asleep in the middle of the lake was a mistake, though. We woke up drifting alongside some surprised-looking naked women bathing by the banks.

Dusk marked the great exodus of tourists out to Sunset Point, about two kilometres north of Abu centre. 'Oh look,' said Anna as we joined the swaying masses. 'We can go there by camel!' And indeed, two camels were parked at the pony-rank at the bottom of Sunset Road, apparently waiting for us. 'You won't get any argument from me,' I said as money changed hands. 'I don't believe I can walk another step today.'

Anna really enjoyed her camel ride. It made up for her missing Jaiselmer and Khuri. And as we swayed up to Sunset Point atop our noble steeds, we found ourselves the centre of attraction. 'I think we're the only Westerners in town!' said Anna as thousands of local holidaymakers began pointing at and greeting us. 'I feel like Lawrence of Arabia being welcomed into Jerusalem!' I laughingly replied.

The Abu sunset was absolutely beautiful, though not exactly a tranquil experience. Myriad hordes of Indians – *what* a friendly lot they were! – clamoured to 'know' us and have photographs taken with them. Every raised knoll or platform were packed with happy, grinning faces, all waving and beckoning that we come over and join *their* party. Many of them were so busy doing this that they quite forgot about the sunset.

Back in our hotel room I collapsed. Then, reflecting on the day's events, I compiled a short report for Paula:

Rajasthan's only hill-station lies on a 1200 metre high plateau, in pleasantly green and lush surroundings. Principally a place for pilgrimage – holy dips in the waters of Nakki are held to be as spiritually purifying as bathing in the Ganges – it has recently come up as a summer retreat for honeymooning Indian couples (mainly from nearby Gujarat) and is strongly geared to home tourism. The sight of Indians abroad – laughing, joking, taking endless photographs, generally having a ball – has Western visitors completely mystified. It's not like India at all. It's not even like an Indian hill-station – there's no hassle, no dirt, no drugs and no unemployed refugees. The very worst (or best) thing that can happen to you at Abu is being adopted by an Indian family and deluged with food and presents throughout your stay. They just love foreign tourists here, partly because they see so few of them. And their cordiality and friendship is genuinely infectious.

In the evening, Abu came into its own. Looking out the window, I could see sweet buns, ice-creams, 'genuine Bombay omelettes' and ice-cold beers being peddled by the roadside, and the town streets were a mass of gaily twinkling electric lights. 'I was going to bed,' I told Anna as I took in the festive party atmosphere. 'But now I'm going to have one of Abu's famous *pau bhajis*. They're just like Bombay *chaat*, but with a buttered toasted roll thrown in.' Anna turned her nose up at the savoury snack (her stomach was still too sensitive for spicy food) but she did share a DROUGHT BEER with me and had an attractive *mandi* henna pattern done on one her hands.

While we were out, we stopped at the curiously named CHARACTER BUILDING WORLD SPIRITUAL MUSEUM below the tourist office. Here an uninvited guide showed us round a strange exhibition depicting the evolution of the world. Then he told us how ‘Godfather Shiva’ would manage things after it had been blown up.

Chapter 25

Strangers in Paradise

The following couple of days were an improvement, probably because we were in constant movement. In 32 hours, we travelled the entire length of Gujarat, starting at Mt Abu at 7.30am (six hour bus to Ahmedabad) and finishing up the next morning at Diu, at the southern tip of the state.

At the same time, things suddenly eased up between Anna and me. Mainly, I suspect, because we buried our differences and made a subconscious effort to chant together – and to work together. This would be essential since we were heading so far off the beaten track that to do otherwise could have been downright dangerous.

'Why are we going there again?' asked Anna, studying a map.

'It's the final piece of my master-plan,' I grinned in reply. 'Gujarat is virgin territory. Even Lonely Planet have only thinly reported on it. We'll be like strangers in paradise!'

But paradise had a rocky start. As soon as we arrived in Ahmedabad, the capital of the state, we decided we didn't like it. 'Where's the "handsomest town in Hindoostan" lauded by the British envoy Thomas Roe?' I complained, taking in all the grey, anonymous buildings and seething traffic. 'All I can see is another noisy, polluted, and overcrowded Delhi!'

'It is a bit grim and smelly,' agreed Anna.' Do we have to stay here tonight?'

'No, we don't,' I told her firmly. 'And I'm going to make sure of it.'

It was a difficult promise to keep. For one thing – shock horror – hardly anyone appeared to speak English. For another, when I finally found someone in the railway station who did, I was told that the Somnath Mail – the night train to Veraval – was cancelled. Third off, it was a Sunday and we couldn't check this with the (closed) tourist office in the station. 'Okay,' I told Anna even more firmly. 'I'm going to chant about this. *Someone* must know about these bloomin' trains!'

My stubborn, persistent nature came into play. I went to a dozen different railway officials, badgered them into submission by showing them all my 'press' credentials, and eventually established that not only was the Somnath Mail going tonight (it had been cancelled *yesterday)* but a second train, the Girnar Express, was also going to Veraval and would get us there three hours quicker. At the end of this maze of people – all with conflicting information – I returned to Anna waving two tickets in the air. 'There you go,' I said with a triumphant grin. 'Paradise here we come!'

With a whole afternoon to kill before the train left, we decided to escape the simmering heat and cool off in a cinema. Unfortunately, it being a holiday, everybody in town had the same idea. The only movie house without a long queue outside was the 'Advance' in Relief Rd. 'What's on offer?' Anna called to me as I left our auto-rickshaw to investigate. 'It's called *Sex Moments – I'm having a Baby,'* I called back. 'It appears to be an educational film for pregnant white chicks.' Bypassing other dubious films like *Women of a Prehistoric Planet* and *She is a Sexy Cave Girl,* we came at last to a flea-pit showing an enjoyable comedy called *Amar Akbar Antony* with Amitabh Bacchan – Bollywood's current heart-throb – as a bad boy adopted by a priest and transformed into a repentant Catholic. 'This is more like it!' giggled Anna as he leapt out of a giant Easter egg and began apologising to Jesus.

The night train out of Ahmedabad was unexpectedly pleasant. First we got adopted by an Indian family – the father rose from his bunk to feed us chapatis and mango pickle – then everybody went to bed. 'It's only 10pm and they're all asleep,' I whispered over to Anna. 'This is the quietest Indian train I've ever been on!'

Due to the unbelievable silence on this train, both of us slept for a solid eight hours. Then, after chanting in our seats, we chatted pleasantly to our fellow travellers till arriving in Veraval at 10am. From what I had seen out the train window, Gujarat – or this part of it at least – was a vast, largely unpopulated, tract of rich, green, arable territory on which nothing (except the occasional pair of bullocks lazily ploughing up fresh sets of furrows) stirred. 'No wonder Gujarat is so well-off,' I told Anna as I took in mile upon mile of freshly-tilled corn, grain, and banana crops. 'Like Kerala, it has such an industrious, hard-working farming community who have developed the land and brought forth its full fruits. As for the Gujaratis, they seem to be either well-educated, smartly-dressed businessmen like we saw back in Ahmedabad or simple farming folk out here in the sticks, the men dressed in the traditional little white caps and smock-type frilly shirts.'

'There's also a third category,' added Anna later as we stood at Veraval's hot and dusty bus stand. 'We've been waiting for 40 minutes for a bus on to Oona, and in all of that time we've been stared at by incredulous locals, mainly squat, swarthy fisher-folk. I don't think they see many foreigners.'

Having survived the bumpiest bus in India – the two and a half hour local bus to Oona – we boarded another bus the final 10 kilometres to Ghoghla, then took a ferry across the bay to our final destination – the small ex-Portuguese island of Diu.

'Phew! It reeks of fish!' was Anna's first comment as we

stepped off the ferry.

'Well, what do you expect?' I said with a laugh. 'As a coastal fishing-town, most of the population make their living from the sea.'

Our first port of call was the tourist office, 200 yards up from the ferry jetty. But there was no tourist officer. 'He out of station,' said one of his morose assistants. 'He go Nagoa Beach.' Anna thought I'd be depressed about this piece of news, but I wasn't. 'Ah ha,' I told her. 'If the tourist officer goes there, Nagoa *must* be good!'

And indeed it was. At Nagoa, a short rickshaw ride away, we finally came to paradise. Not only did we find the best hotel we'd been in – the heavenly Ganga Sagar Guest House – but also the best beach in India. An idyllic spot, Nagoa was a long, crescent-shaped stretch of white, clear sands nestling within a quiet, protected cove, fringed by swaying palms and facing onto the Arabian Sea. 'This is perfect!' exulted Anna. 'I'm going for a swim!'

We instantly stripped off and dived into the sea. It was glorious. Then, having washed all the dirt of travel off us, we enjoyed some good simple food back at the lodge. 'Can your stomach handle FISH EMBRYO?' I asked Anna as I studied the menu. 'I think that's caviar,' she smiled in reply. 'A girl can *always* handle caviar!'

But she couldn't. Five minutes after trying it, she threw it up again…right next to the guest instruction saying VOMITING OR ANY UNHYGIENIC THING WILL BE LIABLE TO FINE.

'Oh dear,' I thought to myself as I held her close and tried to comfort her. 'No sooner have we found paradise than it's a case of paradise lost.'

*

Anna was very upset the next morning and I couldn't blame her. She was almost at the end of her stay in India and she'd had no holiday, just an ongoing series of crises – physical, emotional and psychological. I had to hand it to her for stamina and persistence, though. She'd lost an incredible amount of weight, was burnt black by the sun, covered in mosquito bites, but was just getting the hang of this country.

Leaving her in the capable hands of Haridas Samji, our friendly hotel manager, I ventured forth into Diu, to buy a couple of bus tickets back to Bombay. Anna would be going there the following morning to catch her flight back to England. I still had work to do, so would be staying on a few days more.

I found Diu a tidy, neat and attractive town. Like Panjim in Goa, it retained much of its old Portuguese charm – the clean, cobbled streets, the pastel houses, the colourful fishwives in the elegant market square, and the general laid-back, relaxed atmosphere. Everything about Diu was pleasantly Mediterranean.

Except, that is, for the Goa Travels agency opposite the ferry jetty. 'Bus to Bombay full,' said the rude, unhelpful manager. 'It full for rest of week.'

I could not believe this. How was I going to break the news to Anna?

Very fortunately, I didn't have to. The tourist officer was in that day and he told me there was another bus leaving daily for Bombay, but from Ghoghla. He said he'd try and get me tickets and asked me to come back at 4pm.

There followed three of the most nail-biting hours of my life. Being strangers in paradise was one thing. Being stranded in paradise was quite another. If the bus didn't happen, I was looking at packing Anna off to Veraval tonight and hoping she'd be let on the 7.50am train to Bombay without a ticket. I was also looking at cancelling the rest of my tour of Gujarat and joining her. My return flight to England was non transferable and until (if!) Paula wired more money over I could be stuck in India without two rupees to rub together!

To distract myself from this worry, I hired a bicycle and made a hot and rather sweaty tour of the small island. There wasn't much to it, actually – just the old bastioned fort (completed 1547) from which the Portuguese controlled Diu until it returned to Indian rule in 1961, and three old Catholic churches. With so few people of Christian faith remaining, these places of worship had been turned into respectively a school, the town's hospital, and – most peculiar of all – a badminton club. I walked into the last one to find two sporty Indians in Fred Perry T-shirts knocking shuttlecocks back and forth in the cathedral nave.

But it was the almost complete lack of infrastructure – no luxury hotels, no sightseeing tours, no entertainments, no airport, and only three auto rickshaws on the whole island – that got me. 'Blimey', I thought as I rode back to town. 'This must be like Goa was twenty years ago!

At 4pm precisely – and this was unusual in a country where time was so elastic – the tourist officer bounced back into his office. 'Wow,' I congratulated him. 'You come in U.K. time, not India time!' He laughed. 'My father is military man, he wake me and my brothers at six each morning. "Hands off cocks and pull up socks!" he is saying. Oh, and good news – I have your bus tickets!'

Back at Nagoa, and much relieved, I found Anna well on the road to recovery. So much so, that she had held down a meal of omelette and chips, and was now working on the local 'country wine' gin. 'It's typical,' she said ruefully. 'I've had a lovely day swimming and sunbathing, and am finally ready to enjoy India, and I've got to go home!'

It was strange. Over the past few days, I had felt the weight of travelling with Anna lifting. I had in fact come to enjoy her company and to look forward – as I had with Kevin – to sharing each new day's events with someone else again.

I was really going to miss her.

*

'Are you going to be alright?' I asked Anna as we boarded the 10.30am 'disco' bus to Bombay the next day and I hitched a lift with her as far as Oona. 'I will be when they turn this disco music off!' she shouted in reply. 'It's frightening!' And indeed it was. The prospect of 22 hours of this ahead of me in a couple of days was daunting, to say the least.

Anna looked surprisingly calm and positive when I left her at Oona. I guessed that either she had managed to block out the worst of the music with earplugs, or that she had risen through her many trials to the sublime state of Buddhahood– where nothing, absolutely nothing, could disturb her. I had to be impressed.

I was not impressed by the information I got at the small, wooden ticket office at Oona bus-stand. 'No Somnath bus till 6pm,' said the sleepy occupant. 'You come back 6pm.' This was terrible news. By the time I reached Somnath – a long 2 hour bus journey away – everything would be closed. But then I kept asking around and the first bus that came along turned out to be the 12 noon 'express' going there!

Gujarati truck drivers, I noticed on this bus, had a completely different set of hand signals to their counterparts up north. Here, they gave a beckoning wave when it was safe to pass, a downward stab of the hand when it was not safe to pass, and a jiggling cupped-hand motion when it *might* be safe to pass, but if it wasn't, well, ho hum, it was a good day to die. A fourth signal came into play in even more extreme circumstances This was employed not by the truck driver but by his panic-stricken mate sitting in the cab next to him. It was a manic fluttering of the hand out of the window—suggestive of a sparrow caught in a jam-jar—and it meant: 'Slow down for God's sake, or there's going to be a three-vehicle pile-up with us as the meat in the sandwich!'

I liked Somnath to start with. Again, I was the only white face in town, but that pleased me enormously. 'I can't see Lonely Planet sending anyone here in a hurry,' I silently exulted. 'This is the least touristy place I've ever come across.' Strolling down the quiet, narrow lanes full of local traders selling tiny stocks of vegetables or tailors making up clothes on vintage sewing machines or young lads slicing betel nuts for *paan* with what looked like giant hedge trimmers, I came to the main attraction – the ancient Somnath Temple.

Home of one of the 12 sacred *jyotolingas* (Shiva shrines), Somnath was, I had read, the richest temple in all India by the 6th century AD. Its wealth was so great that when the acquisitive Mahmud of Ghanzi descended on it in 1024, even a vast caravanserai of elephants, camels and mules couldn't take it all away. Over the following 700 years, Somnath Temple went through a rash of being built up, knocked down and rebuilt again. Finally, after Aurangzeb (the Moghul iconoclast) did a thorough job on it in 1706, the builders gave up and all that remained today was a 1950 restoration – a decidedly unimpressive attempt at a modern Hindu temple incorporating traditional styles.

To say I was disappointed in this temple would be an understatement. The ground floor 'museum' was just boring bits of rock and a collection of holy (and not so holy) waters in little bottles collected from famous rivers all over the world. The museum on the second floor – a photographic exhibition describing the history and archaeological background to the seven versions of Somnath temple – just left me feeling short-changed by the present one. Slipping over to the upper balconies, with their regal (now extinct) Oriyan lion carvings, I could see that the temple had a magnificent location, overlooking the Arabian Sea and a long stretch of beach. But it was a grey, unshaded beach with nothing and nobody on it.

I could also see from this vantage point that Somnath was very undeveloped at present. Yes, the tour buses were starting to trickle in (so the Diu tourist officer had told me) and zillions of pilgrims apparently turned up from all over India for the big Maha Shivratri festival of February-March, but otherwise it was deadsville. In town, there was only one restaurant to speak of (serving mainly thali meals) and only one hotel – the Hotel Mayuram on Triveni Road. As for the beach, there was nowhere to stay or eat at all. 'Somnath reminds me a lot of Puri,' I reported to my Walkman. 'Except that it's a lot harder to get to and not half as much fun.'

Suddenly, I stopped the tape. 'Why on Earth am I reporting on this place?' I thought in horror. 'Try as I might, I can't think of one reason why anyone – especially monied Westerners – should come here. And the same goes for Diu, except for Nagoa Beach. No wonder Lonely Planet are so silent on Gujarat – it's just not geared to tourism yet!'

I caught a bus to my next destination, Sasan Gir, with a heavy heart. If this largest – and apparently finest – wildlife sanctuary in India was a bust, I'd be filled with regret.

My main regret would be that I had missed the famous Rat Temple in Bikaner.

'Dear Frank,' read a letter I'd picked up from Megan in Jodhpur. *'I see from your itinerary that you're headed for Gujarat. DON'T GO THERE. Go to the Karni Mata temple in Bikaner instead. It's a scream! I visited on the best day – Sunday – when hordes of holiday pilgrims turned up, accompanied by clanging temple bells and crazed drum-playing musicians. I was less lucky visiting at the breeding season – hardly had I taken my socks off than I was literally ushered in on a moving carpet of rats! The central sanctum, presided over by a pair of bowing priests and a dish of feeding rats, was a tiny mini-temple of pure marble with pure silver gates, dating back to the 15th century. The big thing here was to spot the one and only white rat on the premises. This was considered very lucky indeed and was so rarely seen that even the standard postcard of the rats sold across the road had one of the brown species crudely painted over in white! Imagine*

then, the reaction of my taxi driver when I casually pointed out THE white rat to him. There it was, minding its own business, nibbling at a stray bit of rice in a corner. He instantly fell to his knees and began howling gratitude to the skies. Apparently, this sighting—his first in over 50 visits—guaranteed him, his family, and several generations to come the protection of the most powerful saint that Rajasthan has ever produced. The nearest western equivalent, I guess, would be a Catholic getting a personal visitation from the Pope!'

Oh, and that's not the end of it. Outside the temple, and directly opposite, there's a new museum where you can see a gallery of quaint paintings depicting the life of the goddess Karni—all the way from her birth in 1444 to her surprisingly late demise, 150 years later, in 1595. Walking round the 'museum', you can marvel at her major miracles—curing a disfigured aunt by punching her in the head, feeding an entire army with a bowl of curd and bread, restoring a lot of dead locals to life, breaking various others out of jail, saving a drowning merchant whilst calmly milking a cow, and—my personal favourite—miraculously nailing back the disjointed leg of a camel.'

Yes, I thought as I left another grubby thumb mark on Megan's much-perused missive, I would definitely regret not seeing *that*.

*

The main attraction at Sasan Gir was the Asian lion – a magnificent beast averaging a full 2.75 metres (9 feet|) in length and with a larger tail tassel, bushier elbow tufts and more prominent belly folds than his African cousin. A sighting of one of these would, I felt sure, knock a quasi-mythical white rat out of the ball park. But, as at Somnath, I was to be disappointed. 'Now is off season,' said Mr Barbi, the Forest Ranger, as I strolled into Gir village and came upon him playing table-tennis in his Forest Lodge. 'Lion, he is sleeping.' I asked if I could hire a bicycle to go see the sleeping lions, pointing at the row of hire bikes at reception, and he said, 'No, you must take guide. If you want to come home in one piece, that is.' I opened my mouth to enquire how much an accompanying guide and bicycle would cost, but then the slim, bearded man remembered some urgent appointment and left. Not to be seen again that night.

Oh well, his assistant gave me lots of useful information and my room at the lodge was the best I'd ever had – for 20 rupees I got a huge double-bedded chalet with mosquito nets, spotless sheets and immaculate shower-room. Even the walls were lily-white! 'There must be a catch to this place,' I thought as I drifted comfortably off to sleep. 'What could it be?'

My answer came at about 6am. A snuffling sound, accompanied by a low growl, roused me from my slumbers. 'What's that?' I yawned, rubbing my eyes awake. 'Am I having a dream?'

Well, no, I wasn't. Looking over to my (open) window, I saw two enormous paws balanced on the sill and an equally enormous head, framed against the moonlight for even more enormous effect, peering in. 'Bugger me!' I shrieked. 'It's a lion!'

Mr Barbi didn't know what hit him as I rushed out and banged on the door of his private residence. 'Let me in! Let me in!' I cried in blind panic. 'There's a lion on the loose!'

A throaty chuckle issued from within the dark building and then all the lights came on and Mr Barbi issued forth in his dressing gown. 'Oh,' he said jokingly. 'I see you have met

Princess.'

'Princess? What Princess?'

'I am so sorry, my good fellow. She is my pet lady lion. I personally raise her from baby cub. She normally sleep with me. Did you perhaps leave some meaty titbits in your room?

'The only meaty titbit in my room was *me!'* I responded hotly. 'You can't let a lioness with a snack-attack wander around at large. I've heard of them running up a tree with a full grown stag in their mouths. I don't want to die up a tree!'

My unflappable host's response was classic. 'Next time I give you upper floor room. Now, come, since you are up, let me show you my vultures.'

Mr Barbi's vultures lived in a large covered crate outside the lodge and they were *huge.* 'My God,' I said with more than a hint of alarm in my voice. 'How did you get them in there?'

'Military personnel,' replied Mr Barbi. 'They shoot them down with tranquilliser. They are putting holes in too many low-flying aircraft.'

All of a sudden, my earlier note into my Walkman – that Gujarat would be far more attractive when commercial flights started coming in – didn't sound so attractive any more. 'Does this kind of thing happen very often?' I asked Mr Barbi nervously, and he said, 'Oh yes. Soon we will be needing bigger cage.'

Mr Barbi next introduced me to his pride and joy – the Crocodile Breeding Centre just below the bus stand. Here, in a pleasant green compound, lived around 700 sleepy crocs ranging in size from 13 centimetres (5 inches) to 1.5 metres (5 feet). 'The number of marsh or 'mugger' crocodile go suddenly down some years back,' he explained. 'So now we collect eggs from nearby Kamleshwar Dam, bring them here to be artificially hatched, then release them into natural habitat.

What you think?'

There was a brief pause as I considered my response and then Mr Barbi got bored and decided to play a practical joke on me. 'Take good photo!' he laughed, reaching down and casually tossing a baby crocodile at me. 'Good for holiday album!'

I had never been so discombobulated in my life. 'Eek!' I said as I found myself juggling a six inch crocodile between both hands, and then 'Ouch!' as two of its 66 baby teeth chomped into my left thumb. Mr Barbi found the whole thing most amusing – especially when I fell into a whole pit of the wriggling little monsters and had an Indiana Jones moment fighting my way out again.

With my humour now quite ruined, and with nothing else to see in Gir, I returned to Diu via an enervating series of bus journeys. And found my peaceful oasis of the Ganga Sagar Guest House now occupied by a sulky Frenchman ('Do not bother me. I am seeing the sea') and a rowdy holiday party of Indians on the top floor. I moved rooms three times to escape the noise and ended up downstairs, in a poky little annexe.

It was with mixed feelings that I recalled the day's events. It had been profitable, but I felt edgy and restless to be back in the U.K. in front of my typewriter. Sixty-two days down the line and with only four more to go, I had pretty much reached the end of my research. But what had I actually written? Hardly anything! It had been okay for Steve, sitting up there in his holiday home in Manali. He'd had all the time in the world to pen his pensive reports on North India. All that I'd managed to do was dash around the whole continent like a headless chicken – pecking up information without regurgitating much out again. My mind went back to my most recent letter from Paula: 'Loved your reports on Jaiselmer and Mount Abu…but where's the rest of it?

I had no answer.

Chapter 26

Bombay or Bust

The following day was the 'big push' down to Bombay, and I was dreading it. My short time on the Bombay bus with Anna had really put the willies up me. 'Got the earplugs against the booming disco music?' I did a mental resume. 'Check! Got the inflatable cushion for the inevitable bum-crunching bumps in the road? Check! Got the crash helmet for when we hit a particularly deep pothole and I am jettisoned out of my seat and into the luggage rack? Oh dear, no check!'

I made the M.T.C. bus stand in Ghoghla with ten minutes to spare, sweating like a pig. Not only had the rickshaw I'd ordered out of Diu failed to appear (I had to hitch a lift from a passing Public Carrier), but the ferry to Ghoghla was late and then I'd had to walk the whole way from Ghoghla jetty to the bus stand with my heavy bag on my head in 40 degrees of heat. Everybody in town was vastly amused.

Once on the bus, I was amused too. 'This is promising,' I commented into my Walkman. 'The bus seems to have three drivers. No, I correct myself: two drivers and a personal window cleaner!'

The only driving I saw driver number one do was when the bus revved up and taxied out of Ghoghla in first gear. Two hundred yards down the road, it stopped and driver number two slid into place. Driver number one started making up his bed, and driver two started reversing back up the road. Obviously, only one of the drivers was qualified to drive *backwards.* As for the window cleaner, his agitated rubbing circular motions against the window left me in no doubt as to his occupation. I was very impressed by this window cleaner. One moment, he was lounging about in the door like an SAS man waiting for the word; the next, he was gone! I didn't actually see him go, but all of a sudden he wasn't there. Then, about ten minutes later, he stepped back into the bus…from outside! He'd been outside the bus, travelling at about 60 miles an hour, and I could only assume that he'd been right round the bus – holding onto the handles of the windows and giving them all a quick wash-down.

I was less amused in Oona, where the bus stopped for a whole hour and a lot of extra passengers got on. It soon became apparent that the bus had been double-booked, so that 7 people had to sit for 22 hours in the gangway on little steel seats. 'My God, those poor sods,' I thought in horror. 'How *awful!*'

It was an incredible journey. I had chanted that the video TV screen over the driver's head would break down. Well, it did, but so did the bus. Three times. Twice for punctured tyres, and finally – because driver one slept on top of the air filter, so that it overheated – when the generator broke down. The collective effect of all this was that we arrived in Bombay five hours late. And most of the journey, I was jostling for possession of my arm-rest with some farting, sneezing, coughing, nose-blowing old Gujarati who periodically collapsed to sleep on the floor (he was one of the unlucky ones perched on stools in the aisle) and then crept off it like a moaning, creepy zombie, laying a spidery hand on my arm each time to raise himself back into the land of the living.

Spending 27 hours on a video bus with a load of Indians who didn't speak a word of English was no joke. The only thing that kept me sane was that knack – perfected back on the Jammu/Manali run – of going into mental 'stasis', of going hours in a suspended animation trance state where time had little or no meaning. This became much easier when my elderly Gujarati neighbour fell to the floor again around 5am and just stayed there.

'Now, what was the only marathon bus journey worse than this one?' I thought during one of my mind's brief meanderings. 'Oh yes, it was the Magic Bus back in 1977. It should have got me from London to Athens in 36 hours. It took five days. It took five days because the driver was drunk and the bus had a missing wheel and a leaking fuel tank. A second (sober) driver with a better bus materialised on day three, but he had no idea where he was going. We drove around Austria in circles for a further day, until the driver was forced to buy a road map from a ramshackle gas station on the outskirts of Villach. We reached Athens on the evening of day five with one of our number trying to throttle the driver in his seat, and him shouting: 'I am not responsible! This is first time I am driving outside Poland!'

During another brief meandering, I fell to reflecting on David Lean's film *A Passage to India.* In particular, on the heroine's parting comment as she set sail for England after her Indian adventures. 'I must come again,' she wistfully remarked. 'There's something else I haven't seen. I don't know what exactly, but I know it's there!' I gave a brief nod of agreement and in my mind began composing a short introduction to my upcoming guidebook. 'India is *addictive,*' I told my potential readers. 'Once it's got into your bloodstream, there's no getting it out. Nobody returns unaffected or unchanged. You'll never fully understand it and you'll never see it all, but the compulsion to keep trying is what sends so many travellers back again and again.'

There were exceptions, of course, I corrected myself. Kevin was an exception. Kevin couldn't get on with India at all. It brought him out in a rash – a very embarrassing rash in the region of his private parts, caused by a surfeit of caustic soap left in his underpants by local washer men or *dhobis.* His parents were most touched at the tears in his eyes when they met him at the airport on his return. But he was overcome not by emotion, but by 'dhobi itch', and he dived immediately for a chemist who could supply the Whitfields ointment to sort it out. India also, I smiled in recollection, brought out in Kevin a rash of distemper, a manic allergy to carpet salesmen and oily rickshaw men. Back home, everyone commented on how aggressive India had made him.

After the generator packed up, I did an *ushitora* (2am) *gongyo* on a urine-soaked lay-by buzzing with mosquitoes. It must have been a very special cause, because the bus immediately righted itself and we had no further delays at all. Most important, I even learned to *respect* the video bus. I began (albeit with the muted effect of earplugs) to really appreciate the value of loud, jolly songs to help pass the long journey. Also, the one video film shown was so dull that it actually sent me to sleep.

*

By the time I arrived in Bombay, I was absolutely filthy. 'I need a shower,' I thought grimly. 'Thank Buddha I've got a free 5-star hotel lined up.'

Only trouble was, I wasn't exactly 5-star hotel material. Not only was I very smelly and very stressed out but I had…ahem…rather let myself go in Gujurat. I now sported a golden hoop in my left ear from Pushkar, a ratty old T-shirt with 'Just say Yes' from Manali, a grimy *holi* scarf round my head from Delhi, and a pair of beaten up sandals from Jaiselmer.

The tall, turbaned Sikh guard at the door of the Taj Continental hotel was not impressed. 'We do not allow hippies,' he said, his lip curled in a sneer.

Hippy? Moi? Well, I wasn't having that. With a grunt of displeasure, I swept him aside, plunged into the hotel's vast lobby, and howled – with all the anguish that two days of little sleep and hardly any food could muster – 'I am *not* a hippy! I am a *travel writer,* for God's sake!'

Fortunately, the nice P.R. lady who had welcomed me into India two months earlier spotted me and called off the pursuing Sikh.

'There, there, Mister Queasy,' she said calmly. 'You'll feel better after a long, hot bath.'

'I don't want a long, hot bath!' I raged, still quaking in her lobby. 'I want that man *sacked!'*

'We'll talk about that in the morning, Mister Queasy. Oh, and do me a small favour. Lose the earring, will you…'

That poor man. I really shouldn't have vented my spleen on him. He had only been doing his job. I should have remembered – the hotel had a strict dress code and I had most definitely crossed it.

The suit that the P.R. lady loaned me changed everything. It was a very nice suit, and I was surprised—no, *amazed*—at the difference it made in the way Indians treated me. I was *so* amazed indeed, that I expanded the 'What to Take' section of my book by a whole page to extol the merits of 'the suit':

If you're planning on a luxury holiday—staying in big modern hotels or plush heritage properties—a suit for men and a swish evening dress for women is 'de rigeur'. Unlike in Thailand, where you can walk around in just about anything and not be judged or pigeon-holed, here in India you are what you WEAR. A certain amount of tolerance is afforded in most deluxe hotels, but a visible sneer can be detected at the reception desks of the snobbier ones. There is nothing more satisfying, in my experience, than turning up looking like an old hippy and emerging, an hour or so later, dressed like a rich yuppie—complete with suit, tie, polished shoes and pressed Italian shirt. It really confuses them, because there is nowhere in the Indian caste system for Westerners to go. We either dress down, which boxes us as tourist out-castes, tolerated only for our dollars, or we dress up, which puts us alongside the new post-war Indian 'business' caste—and therefore entitled to respect. What we as Westerners fail to understand is that even today, a lot of poor Indians will, given the choice, spend their money on a SUIT rather than a TV. It instantly improves their status in society and gives them real identity. By the same token, what many Indians fail to fathom is why we 'rich' foreigners spend a fortune (in their currency) travelling to, and around, their country and wander round in shorts, trainers and T-shirts. Where are the SUITS, they wonder?

The suit opened all sorts of doors for me. Baskets of fruits and sweet-smelling flowers arrived in my room, people phoned me up every few minutes to ask if I was 'all right', staff treated me with fawning deference, room-boys and bell-boys waited on my every word, and the manager insisted on treating me to a slap-up supper.

There was only one problem with the suit. I didn't feel comfortable in it. My neck chafed against the loaned tie, my wrists felt shackled by the loaned cuff links, and my feet pinched in the loaned Gucci shoes. And it was not just the physical discomfort that got to me. I just couldn't handle walking around like a stuffed shirt all the time and having awkward, stilted conversations with 'important' people. I felt like a fraud – a hippy lamb dressed up as high-class mutton.

My discomfort turned into downright depression that night as I tried to sleep in my quiet, air-conditioned suite with posters of Douglas Fairbanks dotted all around it. The bed was too comfortable, the temperature was too cool, and the oppressive silence made me feel like I was lying in a tomb. 'Blow this for a game of soldiers,' I thought after five hours of wrestling with my double-decker duck eiderdown pillows. 'This is not the real India. I'm going back to the City Lodge.'

Chapter 27

A Surprise Reunion

It seemed fitting that the first person I saw back at the City Lodge was Megan. It was almost as though she had been waiting for me.

'I *have* been waiting for you,' said my grinning young friend, leaning forward to peck me on the cheek. 'I had your whole itinerary, remember? But you're a day later than expected. What held you up?'

'Don't ask,' I said, giving her a weary hug. 'I tried to live it up with the rich and famous at the 5-star Taj, but it didn't work out. First they tried to stick me in a suit. Then I had a really bad night's sleep. Then, the final straw, they inflicted the worst room service in India on me.'

The freckles on Megan's nose twitched with amusement. 'Oh, how did that work out?

'Not very well, actually. At 6am, feeling really thirsty, I phoned up room service and said: "I would like four Seven-Ups in my room, without forgetting the bottle opener. Then, half an hour later, I phoned again and said: "Where is my Seven-Ups?" The voice at the other end replied: "Oh, you don't want it. I phone back your room and say we have no more Seven-Ups, and you say you didn't order it." So then, still remaining calm, I suggested: "I think you must have phoned the wrong room, send Limca instead." Twenty minutes passed and I rang back again and he said: "I bring it to your room and you say you don't want it. Finally, having lost the will to live, I asked: "What is my room number?" and he said "201", to which I replied, "no, it's 102, please send immediately!" And whoa, yeah, there it was, in two minutes flat—minus the bottle opener. "Where is bottle opener?" I enquired, and the waiter said: "in your bathroom". So I chased him down the corridor and said: "Nothing in bathroom – kindly point it out to me." He came back *very* reluctantly, searched the whole suite, including lifting up the mini-bar and looking underneath it, and then, having no luck, went off and came back with a *huge* bottle-opener from the kitchen. "This is our personal opener", he declared. "You must open bottles and give me back". Well, I didn't want three fizzy drinks going flat while I drank the fourth, so I said "Thanks" and closed the door on him.'

As Megan helped me with my bags and showed me to my room, she asked the 64 million dollar question. 'So, did Anna enjoy India, then?'

I winced. 'No, not really. She was even more allergic to it than Kevin, and that's saying something. Plus she wasn't too happy hearing about me and you in Darjeeling.'

Megan's eyes widened. 'You told her?'

'Yes, I had to. It was the right thing to do. Besides, it was only the once.'

'Was it?' Megan's eyes now had a mischievous twinkle in them.

'Yes, it was,' I said with more than a hint of regret in my voice. 'Though if I ever find myself stuck up a freezing mountain for the night again, you'll be the first person I call.'

An unspoken look of understanding passed between us. Friends it was, and friends it would always and only be.

'So,' said Megan, changing the subject. 'How did the trip go? Did you have any hiccups?'

'The trip went amazingly well,' I replied, flopping on my thin mattress with exhaustion. 'I just need to catch up on about three days sleep. As for hiccups, didn't you get my letter about Steve?'

'Yes, I did,' said Megan. 'I got it a week ago, when I was in Jodhpur. And I went straight over to that hospital to see how he was doing. He was doing fine.'

'Doing fine?' I said incredulously, throwing off my fatigue and sitting bolt upright. 'I thought he was dying!'

'So did everyone. But then that medic his folks brought over checked him out and pronounced a mis-diagnosis. He didn't have rabies at all. He had cerebral malaria. The two things are often confused, apparently.'

'And he's going to be alright?'

'Yes, he's got a bit of liver damage and some of his brain may be shot, though he personally reckons that might have something to do with all the *ganga* he was smoking in Manali.'

I laughed. 'That Steve. I bet he's sorry he gave me all his tapes and diaries now. Look, I've really got to crash out for a bit. Can we catch up a little later on?'

Megan hesitated in the doorway as though she was about to tell me something, but then thought better of it. 'Sure thing,' she said. 'Catch you later!'

When I awoke it was dark. I looked at my watch. It was close on midnight. I had slept a solid 11 hours. I looked to my left and there was a neat, folded note on my bed stand. *Hi Frank,* it said. *I didn't have the heart to tell you, you looked so tired, but I'm returning to UK today. My taxi is arriving in a minute for the airport. It was so good to see you again, let's catch up when we're both home, okay? Oh, and let me know how the book goes – I'll be your first customer! Love, Megan xxx*

*

There were two amusing incidents as I prepared to leave India. First, just as I was checking out of my room, the hotel's plumber appeared with his tool kit. 'Excuse me, sir,' he asked me. 'Can you leave your room key? I am going to change geyser—there is no flush—so please *do* something in your toilet!'

Second, as I poked my nose out onto the heat-blasted pavement, a small boy ran up and said: 'Hello, smiling sir! Which country is belonging to you?' I said 'What?' And he said, 'Which country is currently missing your presence?'

I found much to enjoy as I drove to the Government of India tourist office to finish my information gathering. I looked one way and there was a taxi with its boot open, packed to capacity with green bananas. I looked the other way and there was a blue-line public bus, with people running alongside it and leaping suicidally aboard while it was still in motion.

Further down the road, blinkered ponies pulling impossibly heavy loads passed by, as did a stream of bell-ringing bicycles with not a single straight tyre between them. Then my rickshaw stopped for a red light and a leper stuck his stumpy, bandaged hand into the cab, begging for alms.

All of a sudden, something in me didn't *want* to leave India just yet. It had been a very short trip—just 66 days—and once more I had barely scratched the surface. What was there for me back in England anyway? Empty highways, no street life, grey characterless buildings, and not a cow or pig in sight. If it weren't for Paula and the ridiculously tight deadline she had set for me, I would have changed my flight and stayed on longer.

Having found the Bombay tourist office far more accommodating this time, and armed with a big bunch of maps and brochures, I returned to the City Lodge to pick up my bags. And found that it had a new sign outside the entrance: OUT SIDERS SHOULD NOT ASK ABOUT CRICKET OR

STAND IN SHOP. I smiled at that. Megan and I had had such fun looking down on the boy cricketers below the hotel at night, with the local howling dogs as irregular 'fielders'.

My final walk along the streets of Bombay was fascinating – pavements and arcades packed with shoeshine boys, 'disco' cassette salesmen, people selling tiny stocks of biros, and stalls peddling padlocks, children's toys, fruit (mainly sliced water-melons, buzzing with flies) and vegetables. Most of these people would, it was apparent, be lucky to earn more than a few rupees a day.

With a couple of hours left to kill, I decided to cool off in one of Bombay's many air-conditioned cinemas. But fate or karma had other plans for me. I met a young Hindu – a happy, carefree soul – who dearly wanted to be a priest. He said this was no problem, there being numerous temples open to people with this ambition. He got up at 5am every morning to open his little temple, to perform all the rituals, to receive all the guests, and to do all his meditations. This carried on till noon. Then he went off to his daytime job at a high-class tailors and beavered away at it all afternoon. The evening, he set aside for relaxation – he would laugh, he would make merry and (because Shiva did it) he would even permit himself a puff on the holy *ganga*. He showed me all the photos of his foreign girlfriends. He didn't seem 'qualified' to be a priest – just lucky enough to be of the right caste, to feel a calling, and to able to follow it. A young man, in his early 20s, he looked like any other ordinary Indian. I didn't believe he *was* a priest until, out of the blue, he invited me to come see his temple. I duly followed on and he welcomed me in and sat me down and we began chatting. A few minutes later, he abruptly leapt up and announced, 'I've got to go now.' Then he went off and began banging a loud gong in his shrine accompanied by a friend waving a candle about in mystic circles. He returned and sat down as though nothing had happened. Curious, I asked him what had. 'Oh,' came his casual reply. 'I was just saying goodnight to Shiva – he goes to bed about this time.'

This experience really touched me. So much so, that when I caught a bus to the airport a few minutes later and a moaning Western tourist began slagging off India, I found myself in passionate disagreement with him. 'I'm sorry,' I said with uncharacteristic fervour. 'But I *like* the Indians. I like their music, I like their hospitality, I like their good manners, and I like their country. I've been treated with nothing but kindness since I got here. If India has been less kind to you, then I think you've got a problem!'

'Goodness,' I thought to myself as I came to the end of my rant. 'Where did that come from?' And then the penny dropped. All this time, without realising it, my feelings about India had been changing. From an alien dropped on a different planet when here last year with Kevin, I was no longer an amused observer but a fully engaged participant in this beautiful, amazing, frustrating, funny, chaotic land of contrasts.

I began planning my trip back.

Postscript

My relief at having survived my 66 day challenge – I actually kissed the tarmac when I touched down in Heathrow – was tempered by the even greater challenge ahead. Five days later, I moved out of Anna's cosy little flat and into a far dingier one down the road in Lewisham. With upwards of 70,000 words to write in three months – and my mind too preoccupied with this mammoth task to even say 'Hello' in the morning – it seemed only fair.

'Are you sure you're doing the right thing?' said Anna miserably as I packed my bags to leave.

'It's only three months,' I replied. 'Then we can get back to normal.'

Back to normal? I didn't know the meaning of the word. Little did I know it, but the most chaotic, non-normal, year of my life was on the horizon.

I was about to go off the beaten track…

~ THE END ~

A Message from the Author

To subscribe to my mailing list just paste **http://eepurl.com/bvhenb** into your web browser and follow the link. You'll be the first to know when my next book is ready to be launched!

Hi folks – Frank here!

Thank you so much for reading my book, I do hope you enjoyed it. If you did, I'd love it if you could leave a few words on Amazon as a review. Not only are reviews crucial in getting an author's work noticed, but I personally love reviews and I read them all!

I'd also love it if you checked out my other travel memoirs: *Too Young to be Old* **smarturl.it/TooYoungToBeOld**, *Kevin and I in India* **http://smarturl.it/KevinIndia15** *Off the Beaten Track* **http://smarturl.it/OffBeaten15** and *Rupee Millionaires* **http://smarturl.it/RupeeM15.** Not to mention (though I just did!) my two quirky, award-winning cat books *Ginger the Gangster Cat* **http://smarturl.it/Gingergangster15** and Ginger the Buddha Cat **http://smarturl.it/Ginger15.** Thanks!

Oh, and if you like reading memoirs, there's a really cool Facebook group called 'We Love Memoirs'. We'd love it if you dropped in to chat to the author and lots of other authors and readers here:

https://www.facebook.com/groups/welovememoirs/

P.S. Here's where you can find me on Twitter:
https://twitter.com/Wussyboy

And where to catch me on Facebook:
https://www.facebook.com/frank.kusy.5?ref=tn_tnmn

And if you get the urge, you can always email me:
sparky-frank@hotmail.co.uk

Acknowledgements

Many, many thanks go to these lovely people: Ida of Amygdaladesign (for another amazing cover), Cherry Gregory (for the first beta read and lots of helpful suggestions), to my good friends Julie Haigh and Pat Ellis (for subsequent beta reads and yet more helpful suggestions) and to the "I.T. God" that is Roman Laskowski for just about everything else. Roman, you rock!

A special mention goes to my wonderful wife 'Madge' for her constant support and encouragement. She completes me.

About the author

FRANK KUSY is a professional travel writer with over thirty years experience in the field. He has written guides to India, Thailand, Burma, Malaysia, Singapore and Indonesia. Of his first work, the travelogue *Kevin and I in India* (1986), the Sunday Tribune wrote: “Relentlessly honest, refreshingly uncontrived, this diary really works!”

Born in England (of Polish-Hungarian parents), Frank left Cardiff University for a career in journalism and worked for a while at the Financial Times. India is his first love, the only country he knows which improves on repeated viewings. He still visits for business and for pleasure at least once a year. He lives in Surrey, England, with his wife ‘Madge’ and his little cat Sparky.

Made in the USA
San Bernardino, CA
20 November 2016